Liz,

Thank you so much for inviting me! Those teens at your school are awesome!

A Teenager's Survival
The Siv Ashley Story

God Bless you Liz!

A Teenager's Survival
The Siv Ashley Story

Siv Ashley

Paws and Claws Publishing, LLC
High Point, NC

Book and Cover Designer: Jennifer Tipton Cappoen
Editors: Lynn Bemer Coble, Katie Streit

Published by **Paws and Claws Publishing, LLC**
1589 Skeet Club Road, Suite 102-175
High Point, NC 27265
www.PawsandClawsPublishing.com
info@pawsandclawspublishing.com

ISBN #978-0-9846724-4-8
Printed in the United States

My special thanks to Ms. Katie Streit.
She has helped me with the writing of this book
tremendously. She was able to put things
into words that I would not have been
able to say so eloquently.

Thank you, Katie.
God bless you.

An Excerpt from the Chapter
"A Moment on the Mountaintop"

I stood just below the summit of the mountain. The group of refugees and I hid amongst the trees, waiting for just the right moment to race to our finish line, the Thailand border. Even in the coolness of the night, beads of sweat dripped down my face, and my heart pounded with anticipation and worry. I thought about my brother. *Where was his body now? Had I really left him behind? Was he really dead?* In my upcoming moment of escape, I had precious time. *But could I really believe what the old lady had said?* This was not the time to question myself. This was the time for concentration.

In a few moments, I would run through the forest with the others. Since I was one of the smallest, I would have to be quick to keep up with them. My lack of food already had left me feeling weak and feeble. As if my stomach weren't queasy enough, my recent actions of random hope for redemption had left bile boiling up my throat into my mouth.

I was suddenly jolted from my worrisome thoughts by the sound of a screaming baby. His piercing cries were sure to blow our cover. We would certainly be found if his hungering wails didn't cease. I watched his mother in panicked tears cover the child's mouth with her hand. Her breasts had already gone dry from starvation, and she was no longer able to provide for her young. She did the only thing a mother could do to save her own life. She smothered her baby to death. It was then that our group decided to travel down the mountain. Regretfully the woman wrapped her infant in a tattered piece of cloth and left him at the top of the mountain.

We quickly raced past the banana and coconut trees. Those trees had once meant food and playtime in my life, but as we ran, they filled my heart with devastation. *How had a place that was as beautiful as Cambodia been filled with such foul-souled scum?*

Suddenly I heard a noise. It was a loud, grinding sound that came from the sky. Though different from a seasonal storm, the noise reminded me of the terror that had instilled my surroundings on day one when we were forced to leave our home: the day after the parade. Just then, a helicopter loomed above us, and at that moment, I was sure it would be my last. A package dropped from the helicopter and dozens more packages followed. *Gifts? Could it be?* I watched cautiously as one of the men reached for a package. Just as he held it between his hands, it exploded in a cloud of dust and fire. All refugees who were nearby were blown back several feet. Those weren't gifts. They were grenades.

I couldn't run because I went into a state of shock. With my free land closer than ever, I begged God to help me to survive. Bombs blew apart on both sides of me and exploded those who once led me into these woods into fragments. My ears rang so loudly that I thought surely the explosions had deafened me. With more packages settling all around me and my head throbbing from my broken eardrums, I fell to my knees and began to cry.

I looked into the sky and remembered my father telling me "believe in God and one day you will go to a place called America and you will be free." I began to pray.

Contents

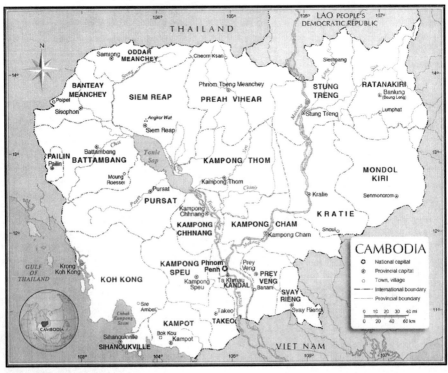

Prologue

Thirty years, and what seems like several dozen lifetimes, have passed since the events that I have described in this book. The following will tell you about my struggles, although I can finally look back with less emotion. The memories of that time are as vivid as if they happened yesterday. I can truly say that my reasons for writing about these experiences were as a testimony to those lives that were lost and for those who can no longer speak for themselves. Oh yes, God was on my side, but I didn't know it then.

In my current world of peace and comfort, I am removed from the horrors of war, the pain of hunger and starvation, and the diseases that caused much suffering, hardship, and even death. However I share the pain, the terror, and the anguish of children, elderly people, and innocent people who have grown up in war-torn countries like Pakistan, Kuwait, and Cambodia.

During the first 13 years of my life, I saw, experienced, and tasted the wraths of war, which will stay with me for eternity. I am hopeful that by sharing my story of war, hunger, suffering, despair, and death, I will shed light on the events that occurred throughout my youth. Eventually I found happiness and a sense of calm. I grew up to live a peaceful life. But it was not always that way.

Everyone says, "This is the stuff that you only see or hear in the movies."

My story is like that of many other Cambodian refugees who were fortunate enough to survive to tell the tale of their hardships, and it is painful and emotional.

Part One:
The Good Years

"The Lord bless thee, and keep thee:
The Lord make his face shine upon thee,
and be gracious unto thee:
The Lord lift up his countenance upon thee,
and give thee peace."
Numbers 6:24–26

Chapter 1
Family and Farm

Fourteen years before my moment on the mountaintop, it was the year 1964. Life was simple for my mother's family then. They maintained a steady lifestyle and lived better than many other families throughout Cambodia. My mother, Ly Pouy Cain, lived at home with her sisters, Ly Pouy Houng and Ly Pouy Mai, and her mother, Ly Cain. She was the oldest of her sisters. My grandfather died when my mother was 15 years old. That put my grandmother in a difficult place, financially and emotionally. She knew that her daughters would have to work twice as hard to help her make a living. It was upsetting to her but also necessary.

My immediate family began in the countryside of Kampuchea, when it was arranged for my mother to marry into a wealthy family. Arranged marriages were a normal occurrence in our country. A woman was married off at a young age to a male who usually lived in another village. Once a woman was married, she would leave her family to join him and his family in his village. Lower middle-class families, like my own, had more options to marry their daughters into wealthier families with higher statuses. To be a middle-class family in Cambodia did not mean life was easy, but it meant that my family was able to eat three meals a day and to make a decent living from the cultivation of rice, and the occasional slaughter of a chicken or pig.

My mother was lovely. Her skin was as white as coconut milk, and her hair was sleek and as black as coal. She had a petite frame; big eyes; a long, pointed nose; and lips that were naturally as red as cherries. These features were favored in Cambodian culture. Paler women with large facial features were considered the most beautiful.

My father, Lum Ba Elle, had heard of my mother's beauty prior to her engagement party, and he decided to invite himself to the event. When he saw her at her engagement party, he instantly fell in love. However, he knew that it was already arranged for my mother to marry into a wealthy family, so his chances of marrying her were slim.

My grandmother did not like my father at first. After all, she had already arranged my mother's marriage with another man, a man who could provide for my mother and give her what she needed to live a rich, full life. However, that man did not love my mother like my father did, and my grandmother grew to learn this. My grandmother had been struggling as a widow for a long time, and she depended on her daughters to maintain living a healthy life. Although the rich man offered wealth, my father offered love and love is something irreplaceable.

After weeks of discussion, my grandmother decided to make a deal with my father. He would be allowed to marry my mother, rather than the rich man with whom the marriage had been previously arranged, if he left his village and joined hers. In Cambodia, this was rare. The woman was supposed to move to the man's village, not the other way around. If my father left his village, he would be seen as a disgrace and his family would be more than disappointed with him. That didn't matter to my father because he knew that he could provide love to my mother. To him, that was all that mattered. So he chose my mother, was disowned from his family, and never spoke of them again. To this day, I have no knowledge of my father's side of the family.

And that is where my story begins. I, Lum Siv Lang, was born in the countryside of Kampuchea, Cambodia, on September 18, 1965. It was such a beautiful place. A tropical forest surrounded my village and the nearby Mekong River supplied our region with water. My life was very suitable when I was smaller, and there were many loving people in my life before the time of war.

I was the eldest with two brothers and two sisters. The people in my life were my parents; my brothers, Lum Maine and Lum Deed; my sisters, Lum Sos Mai and Lum Mai Lee; my grandmother; and my two aunts.

My mother was Chinese. My father was half Cambodian (his mother was Cambodian) and half Chinese (his father was Chinese), so we had a mixed dialect. However, our family primarily spoke Chinese because it was my grandmother's native language. Only about five percent of Cambodians are Chinese descendants. In our language, you always honor the last name of your family first because it helps identify where you come from. A common last name could be traced to a specific village; therefore, the person you are speaking to knows where you reside or where your lineage originated.

My family didn't have much, but we were happy. We lived in a straw-like, one-room house that was constructed from banana tree leaves and branches. It was only about 200 square feet, but it was still big enough to house my family. Our floor was packed-down dirt, and our beds were hammocks that were constructed from tree leaves and trace amounts of twine. We had a small farm where we grew rice and vegetables, and raised pigs and chickens. All of the children were required to help out around the farm. Maine and I could not wait to help out each morning.

During the 1970s, families that were poor were not educated because they didn't have any riels, time, or materials to use to teach. The riel is the currency of Cambodia, which is divided into 100 sen. Four riels are equivalent to $1 in U.S. currency. Therefore, I was never taught to read or write as a child. Neither my grandmother nor my father could read or write. My mother was too busy attending to my younger siblings to teach me anything. It seemed like my mom had a baby each year, and I was always busy helping with them. I didn't mind helping out with my younger siblings though.

Maine and I were the closest out of all my siblings. He was only nine months younger than me. We spent a lot of time together growing up. My family was all I knew other than the seven other families that lived in my village.

We didn't have any toys, fancy clothes, or places to take a nice bath. We waited until it rained to rinse off. All I ever understood about a bath was jumping in the nearby river. We had no indoor plumbing, so our bathroom was the neighboring forest. That was Cambodian life. We made our own homes with our bare hands, and we loved our life because it was the only way of living we knew existed. We were close because of our love for each other.

My mother and grandmother made our clothing, and we had a limited selection of outfits. As a child, I wore handmade underwear and a *sampot* fashioned from a piece of fabric that we traded rice to get. A sampot is a traditional garment of Cambodian men and women that consists of a knee-length, wraparound skirt or sarong.

After my birth, my two aunts were married off and moved away. One day, my aunt who was my mother's youngest sister, Ly Pouy Mai, came back home. She had a little baby of her own cradled in her arms and she was crying, but I didn't understand why. Later on, I learned that her husband had kicked her out of his village because she was "worthless" and "no good to his family." So, as kind as my father was, he accepted my aunt into our home with open arms.

My other aunt, Ly Pouy Houng, married a richer man named Ngoun Chour Sov. She moved in with his family, as established by tradition, unlike my mother who broke away from tradition and did as she wanted. Occasionally, Pouy Houng came and visited us. She brought goodies like candy, cigarettes, and food with her. Since my aunt had married a middle-class man, she was able to give us things that my dad could not afford.

On our farm, we had a couple of pigs, some chickens, and one ox. We bred the pigs and chickens for food and used the ox to help with our garden.

When I was five years old, Maine and I were walking through the forest one day when something hit me from above. I looked up, and there was a monkey hanging from a coconut tree. He continued to throw stuff at us, and it became a game to try and catch him. We couldn't chase him down because he was too fast. Instead, we tried a different strategy. My brother chased him up one end of a small banana tree. When he ran down the other side, I was at the bottom and caught him. I carried the monkey back to our house, and we were careful not to be seen by our parents. He was around seven years old and we named him Tico. Then we had one monkey on our farm. Monkeys were like pets in Cambodia, and they were as common as cats and dogs are in America.

We kept Tico a secret for a long time. When he behaved, he was well hidden, but he acted up too many times. Eventually my dad found out. Dad had been wondering who was stealing the food and was quite angry with us for hiding the monkey. He gave us a small spanking, but he let us keep the monkey. It was fun having Tico for a pet. We had a great time together. He was always my favorite of our animals because he was playful and funny.

Overall, my early childhood was wonderful. We lived a peaceful life and felt safe from harm.

Chapter 2

The River and Rice

There was a little path through the woods to get to the Mekong River, which was about 300 yards away from my house. We went there a few times a day to collect water. There we could bathe, catch fish to eat, and play. Every home in our village used the nearby water source and there was always plenty to go around. We didn't know what water purification was back then, so we just drank the water straight from the creek. I know that this resulted in illness for many, but luckily our family was fortunate enough to stay healthy.

The riverbank and bottom were muddy. It was easy to tell when someone had been there recently because there would be footprints in the mud. We wore no shoes; our bare feet touched the ground. I don't see how I survived through that—running through those thick, branchy woods with bare feet. I guess we were tough.

Part of the river was deep and part of it was shallow. The place we stepped in to get water was deeper, and the place where we played and bathed was shallow. My grandmother didn't go down to the river very much because she was feeble. Since we did not have access to any medical care, it would have been tragic if she fell and was injured. Because of this, she rarely bathed.

After the rainy season, the river would be rushing, but during the dry season it was very still. During the rainy season, the rainfall provided enough water for our crops to maintain a substantial food supply for us during the dry season.

The amount of land you had was related to how much money you had. More land meant that you could grow more food and raise more money. Each household had their own crop, mostly consisting of the same types of food: rice and greens. We had about an acre of farmland to our household, which was enough to provide us with a decent living.

Whatever we could catch—which wasn't much—we would eat. The food we ate most often was rice. We had an abundance of it, and growing our own crop made it easy for us to eat. The other item in our garden was a root-like vegetable that was similar to collard greens. This vegetable was added to every stew, and most meals included it as a side.

My father made sure that we never went hungry. We had rice every day. Some days we shared three fish along with the vegetable. My grandmother usually cooked our meals with the help of my mother. Once in a while, we got a good stew going. On special occasions my dad slaughtered a pig. No part of the pig ever went to waste. We ate the entire thing.

After dinner, my grandmother and mother washed the few dishes we had. My grandmother washed them near the house in a bucket of water we brought, and my mother washed dishes near the river. This applied to our clothing as well. After our clothes were washed, they were hung up over tree limbs. They dried really fast because they were thin and it was hot. Our clothes were either brown or multicolored (reds were most popular).

We didn't have much clothing, but for a little girl, it was okay. We each had a little cloth that we tied around our waists. A little boy tied the cloth in the front, and a little girl tied it on the side. Our parents made underwear, which were small cloth pieces that were tied together, for us. There were a lot of kids who didn't wear anything at all.

The roads were all very narrow and made of dirt. Other than the rice field, which was grassy and drenched with water, brown dirt covered the ground.

Surprisingly, the air always smelled very fresh and clean, and the area was abundantly colorful. The scenery was tropical, and it was incredibly beautiful. Our flowers varied in beauty, and there were coconut trees all around. We had mostly green colors and red colors in our surrounding area, and almost all of the flowers were red. We didn't see much white. There was a little yellow and so much brown dirt. When I was a child, my favorite color was red. I thought all of the red flowers were so pretty. I never really saw the color purple until I moved out of Cambodia. I think that it's my favorite color now.

We didn't live that far from our neighbors. We were only about 300 yards away from them. It was a very small village, and it was home. All the houses were straw like ours, mainly because there wasn't any other material to use. We made our homes from what we had around us to work with. Most houses were constructed of banana tree leaves that we wrapped together.

We knew that not long after dark we should go to bed, and when the sun came up, we rose with it. The rooster in our yard was our alarm clock.

The river and rice were our two best resources. Without them we probably would have starved.

Chapter 3
A New Friend

When the rainy season ended, my father traveled to Phnom Penh, the capital of Cambodia. He returned home with a new baby elephant. I saw him coming down the road walking side by side with her. I was overwhelmed with excitement and my brother, Maine, and I immediately greeted our new friend with petting and praise. We named her Pupu. I hugged my father, thanking him for our new pet.

As we made our daily rounds through our family's rice field, the hot sun beat down on us. Ripping the shucks of rice from their posts and placing them in our baskets was hard work. Pupu had arrived just in time to join us for the end of our harvest, and she carried a small till around on her back. It seemed so effortless for her.

The seasonal rain had provided our region with more water, which made our drinking and bathing water cleaner and cooler. It also provided our rice crops with a much-needed concentration of water. We would eat like kings this week. I led Pupu to the river and she bathed with us. She shook her ears and water sprayed around us like a fountain. I rinsed the day's filth from my face and shook the dirt remnants from my undergarments. This was a common practice for those able to swim and for those who were agile enough to trek through the mud to get to the waterside.

We returned home with pails of water for our family. Maine had spilled most of his, as usual, since he clumsily shifted his container from hand to hand. I was always the more successful one on the water trips. I could balance a large bucket on my head and walk up the trail to home without spilling a drop. I'm not sure when I learned how to do this. It just seemed natural to me.

Pupu ate straw or the leftovers from rice meals. She could hold a whole banana with its peel in her trunk and pop the banana out of the peel and straight into her mouth. Sometimes Tico stole her food, but that usually didn't end well for him. The elephant would flap her ears and scare him off, or she would hit him with her trunk.

Sometimes we rode Pupu in the rice field, which messed up the field more than it helped. Our dad always got mad at us about it, but our mother didn't have much to say. In fact, our mother was always very quiet, and I never heard much from her.

We used the elephant and the ox for tilling the land. Our father had traded various materials to get these animals. He had traded enough rice to get Pupu and the ox had been paid for with the money he had on hand. That was pretty rich for Cambodia; most people only had one animal.

Pupu was very smart. Soon she learned words and was able to respond to basic commands. "Up" was one command I gave her the most often. When I said it, the elephant kneeled and allowed me to climb up her front leg to get on her back. Pupu also wrapped her tail around big logs and dragged them from the field and out of the way. We primarily used those logs for firewood. I don't know what we would have done without her.

Once in a while, Pupu held water for a long time in her trunk. She kept it in there for so long that we didn't realize she had it in her. Then, without warning, she blew the water on us and got us soaking wet. I always thought it was funny, especially when she used this trick on our father.

Pupu followed us to the jungle when we went to collect fruit or to play. She knew how to play hide-and-seek in the woods too, and this was really fun. She blended in with a dark area where there were plenty of banana trees and lots of brush that blocked her from our view. As she grew up, she became easier to spot. Eventually, it was very difficult for her to hide from us, but for then, we loved playing hide-and-seek with her. We loved her from the start, in spite of her occasional, silly playfulness.

Tico occasionally jumped in and played with Pupu. He climbed up on her head and messed with her ears. When he did that, the elephant reached her trunk around and swatted at him, which scared him away. The ox didn't play. He was simply used to till the land.

My dad never beat the animals. "If you treat your animal like you should, it will help you and love you like its own," my father said. He was right. Pupu was very loyal to us. She was our protector, she never let anyone bother us, and she was aggressive toward outsiders.

From playing to working, Pupu was a blessing to have. She entertained us if we ever got bored, and she helped us do the hardest of our work.

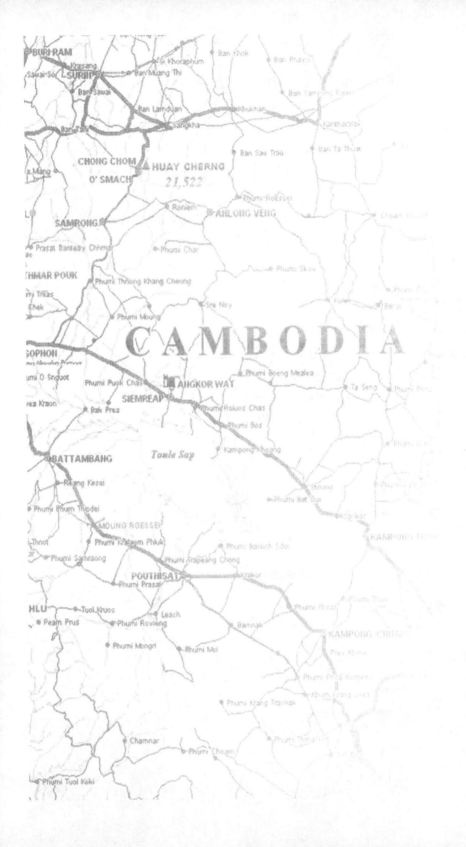

Chapter 4
Campfire Lessons

At nighttime, my dad liked to tell stories. He counted the stars and told us "someday you're going to be there." I couldn't figure out what he was saying because I was young. It has only been in more recent years that I can look back on the events that happened with my father and know that he truly was a very wise man.

We had a fire going on most nights. We roasted little frogs that we caught in a hole. The frogs hid in holes. You always hoped to pull out a frog and not a snake. Grandma always held my little sister on her lap. My aunt played with her baby. Mom quietly sewed.

Sometimes our neighbors came out. If one adult came over, other people would start coming over too.

On most evenings my father found small animals around our village to cook over the fire pit outside. My grandmother used the water to boil a stew, and she always had special herbs she'd gathered from the forest to give the stew flavor and to keep us all in good health.

Around the campfire, my father taught us most of our life lessons. One thing he taught us was to be wary of certain snakes. The forest was very dense, and there were lots of snakes. The ones that we could kill, we would actually eat sometimes. There were pythons in the forest too. For a small child, a python was a scary creature. But we knew to stay away from pythons and that we did.

Once I saw a python in my village. It was squeezing a neighbor man's leg. It squeezed the heck out of that man's leg until his whole body turned blue. We had to close our eyes because the only way to get the man free was to chop the snake off or to chop the man's leg off. My dad didn't want us to see that. It was a big python and it kept wrapping itself tighter and tighter around the man. We didn't have any guns in our village. If we had had one, we could have killed that snake. Dad carried us away. I imagine that the man died. Whenever a snake came into the village, the men had to kill it. If it got away, it might kill somebody else.

Oddly enough, we hardly ever got sick. I only remember getting sick once, and my grandmother would cure us in just a couple of days by making a special mixture of herbs and roots. I do not know exactly what herbs she used, but I'll bet they could still be used to cure all kinds of diseases. Since these remedies were all we had to cure our illnesses, they must have been powerful plants.

If one of us had a cough, Grandmother would make a pot of leaves mixed with certain herbs. When the water was close to boiling, it would steam up past the brim of the pot. The sick person would hold his or her head over the pot, cover his or her head with a blanket, and inhale the vapors. All of the steam would go into his nose and make him feel better.

If you ever got cut or bitten, my grandmother would put some sort of a plant with a special leaf in a bowl, crush it all to pieces, and mash it. Then she put it on the wound. In a couple of days, the wound would heal.

One evening when we had a large campfire, my grandmother told me the story of how I got my name. She said that my name symbolized the rarest flower in all of Cambodia, Vietnam, and Thailand. You could search through the whole forest and find only one.

We usually started our fire before the sun went down, which gave us kids more time to play. The neighbors and their children joined us at the campfire. We kids danced and played small games together. Around these campfires, the elders told stories, riddles, and common legends. The goal of a campfire was to gather the community to establish friendships and to teach the children lessons.

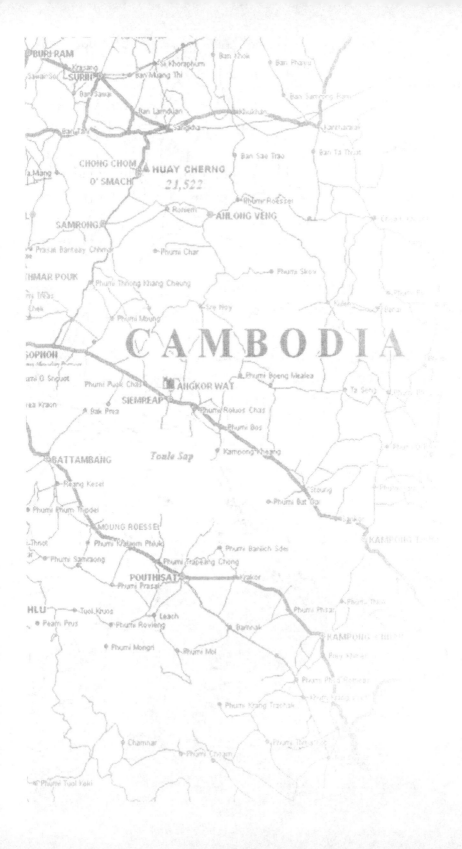

Chapter 5

Bananas

Bananas were another source of food for villagers in my area. The tropical forest surrounding our village was naturally abundant with fruit trees. Bananas were a delicious treat for Maine and me. We went out to the woods and picked bananas straight from the trees. We usually picked bananas from smaller trees to avoid climbing. Tico joined us on most days. He ran ahead of us and climbed larger trees to reach the fruit. Then he devoured the bananas. They were Tico's main source of food.

On days when the harvest was slow, the children in the village all gathered to play. Sometimes we kids took a banana peel and tore it in half. We drew lines in the dirt with sticks and created spaces to jump to and from. We took the banana peel and folded it in three ways. A banana peel was made to look like a rock. Then we threw the banana-peel ball and hoped it would hit the square we wanted. We loved to watch people mess up and to watch people step on the banana peel and slide down in the mud. We had a blast when we played that game.

That was such a carefree time in my life. It's hard to believe that just a few short years later I would face the biggest challenges in my entire life.

Sometimes we climbed up the coconut trees in the wooded area. We sat up there and we watched until someone walked by. Then we threw a coconut at the person's head and took off running. We slid down the tree fast, but they always knew who did it. My dad was the one who punished us and our mom just gave us a look. Dad bent me down, took a bamboo stick, and gave me such a whooping. Your age determined how many times you were spanked. If you were five, you got five spankings. My brother always got a lesser lash. We tried to blame what had happened on each other, but it didn't work. Both of us usually got a spanking.

We played the coconut game with bananas too, but the banana trees were harder to get out of. We were usually caught right away.

Some days I ran off and played with the neighbor kids. We played games like making mud dishes and pretending that we were eating like rich people.

Chapter 6

Believing

My father wanted to provide my brothers and me with an education, so he decided to travel to the capital, Phnom Penh. Our village was far from the capital. It took around a week to travel there by foot. My father took bags of rice with him so that he could get sugar, cloth, and sometimes flour. Rarely he could exchange some rice or our vegetable crop for extra money.

There, he was hoping to trade goods at the store and bring home lots of money so he could send my siblings and me to school. However, the rice and greens my father took to trade lacked significant monetary value, so his time in the capital was mostly spent meeting new people.

In Cambodia, the dominantly practiced religion was—and still is—Buddhism. Over 98 percent of the population practices this religion. We were instructed to pray to a small statue and light incense sticks during this practice. Buddha was a big thing. It was never explained to me why we had to worship him. We just did.

While in Phnom Penh, my father ran into some people who were talking about God. He began listening as they translated whom Jesus was and what God could do for him and his family. My father told them that he believed in Jesus. He found solace in learning about a more promising belief than Buddhism. He wondered how he could pretend to pray to another god, like Buddha, when he believed and trusted in the one, true God. When my father returned home, he was eager to tell us the knowledge he had gained in Phnom Penh.

Late at night, he secretly told us stories about God. We learned that if we told anyone that our faith was different from the Buddhist faith in our region, we would be severely punished, so it was important to keep our faith in Jesus a secret. He told us about how Jesus walked on water and how He fed thousands of people with two fish and five loaves of bread. I was so amazed about everything my dad said that I couldn't wait to hear more each time he came back from Phnom Penh.

From these biblical lessons that my father taught us, I remember him saying, "Remember to call on Jesus if you ever need help. Believe in Him, even though you can't see Him, for He is in your heart. Do this and one day, I believe you will go to a place called America and there you will be free."

Chapter 7

Suzy

One of my greatest memories was the time when my father brought back a gift for me from one of his visits to Phnom Penh. He approached me with a big grin on his face and said, "I've got something for you."

From behind his back he pulled out a little cloth doll. She looked like me, with dark hair and eyes. She wore a small dress and had a painted face and braided hair. I decided to call her Suzy, and she was my favorite gift, toy, and surprise that I ever received.

That made me the first child in our village with an actual toy. Because of this, I was told to share my doll with the other kids in the village. It made me sad that I had to share my toy with the other children, but it was my duty to share because they didn't have any toys.

I carried Suzy everywhere. Tico was always with me too. Sometimes he would hide my doll, which irritated me and made me fear the loss of my beloved toy. My brother and the neighboring kids played with Suzy too. We had small picnics in the dirt and made our typical mud pies out of packed dirt. These were our "rich people's dinners." It was a pleasure to have Suzy join us for our feasts.

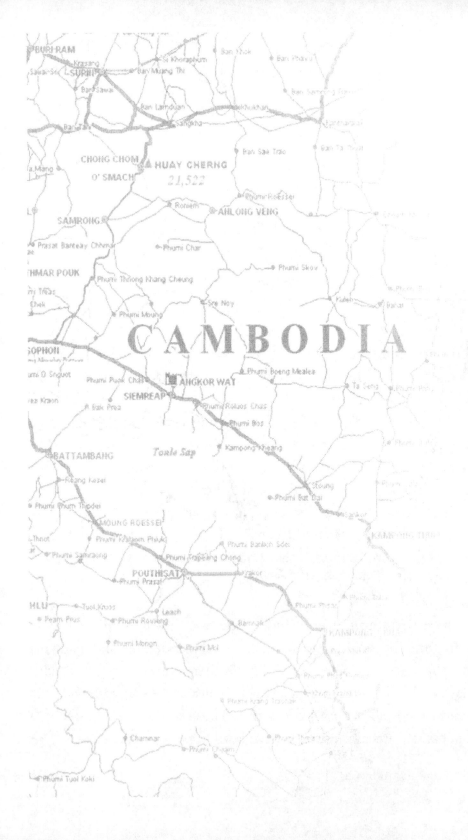

Chapter 8
The Second Village

One day during the dry season my father decided that it would be best if we moved closer to the capital. He thought that this would provide more money for our family and help enable us children to gain an education.

We attached a small wheelbarrow-type cart loaded with our belongings behind Pupu. We didn't have much but what we couldn't fit in the cart was packed on her back. We traveled through little villages and stopped in certain ones to eat, rest, and sleep. We stayed the night with random people. Back then people were very welcoming and trusting of travellers. They even fed us. Along the way, it seemed as though people in each household had the same thing to say: there's nothing near the capital and we were wasting our time. No matter what he heard during our travels, my father was determined that we would have a better life there. Near Phnom Penh, we would learn many new things. My father also remembered the people he had seen who spoke of God and a hope for a better time. He hoped that maybe, just maybe, I could meet some of those people. My father thought that living closer to the capital would give us not only more educational opportunities, but also more spiritual opportunities as well.

Our home in the second village was much different from our home in the first village. The house was made of cement. It was an open area with just one room like our previous home. I don't know if we owned it or if we rented it, but I liked it there. We lived in a more populated area, and I got to see new things that I had never seen before.

There I saw my first bicycle. I thought it was the strangest thing I'd ever seen and it enthralled me. Maine and I immediately asked our father for one, but a bike was completely out of our price range.

New Year's Day was my favorite holiday. I loved that holiday because grandparents put a small amount of money in a little red envelope and gave it to the grandkids. Then we could actually buy something. The coin was smaller than a penny. It had to come in that red envelope. We went to the merchant and saw what we could get from them with the money.

The parade also came around New Year's Day each year. Villages from across Cambodia gathered and created the parade themselves. Participants in the parade were normal villagers. Families paraded through and displayed their oxen or elephants. Oddly enough, it was a legend that stomping on elephant poop would make life better. Both my parents and my grandmother told us that it was considered good luck. So the elephant would walk by and poop, and we would stomp on it with our bare feet. Our parents didn't think it was dirty or gross, because they had learned such legends that had been told to them by their elders. And they hoped to pass on those legends to us.

Children paraded around their neighboring villages carrying their pet monkeys. Women who knew the traditional Cambodian dance, the *Lamthon*, participated in the parade in order to display their talents. The Lamthon features slow, graceful movements of the hands and arms and almost no movement of the feet. Women who danced well or who were of higher class wore decorative *kramas*, which were embellished cloth headdresses.

My aunt, Ly Pouy Houng, came to visit us at our new home. This time, she had a little girl, Ly Hour. We played and played with my little cousin, and when it came time for her to leave, I was upset. My aunt had to go because her husband was good to her and her in-laws were supportive of their marriage. They said that they would allow my aunt to visit us when many other husbands' families wouldn't allow that.

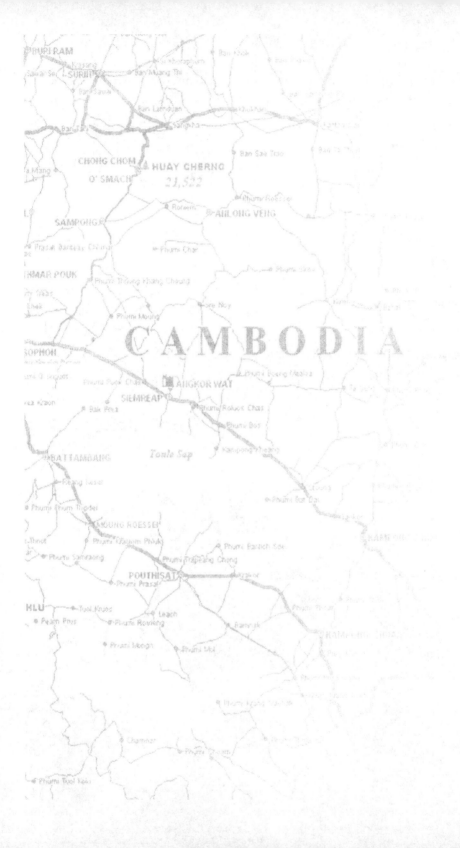

Chapter 9
Kung Fu Fighting

Since we lived in the city, Maine and I would run off to watch kung fu movies. I guess it was kung fu, because they were fighting like crazy in the picture projected on the wall. Dad told us not to go anywhere without permission, but we did anyway. In the theater, we sneaked in without paying for the movie and that was a lot of fun for us. The nearby village had a small *cinema* that attracted a lot of attention from the surrounding village people. Technically, cinema is a much more advanced word than the movie screen that we actually watched there. It was outdoors, and the images from the projector were displayed on a cement wall. The cinema was located in the center of town. A lot of people leaned or sat on the floor. All of us kids liked watching the films because of the action.

One day, we went to see a Bruce Lee movie without permission. My dad came home early that day. When we got home, he was sitting there waiting for us. He did not say a word, but he spanked us so hard that the next day my grandmother let me sit on the pillow. We never did that again.

But we never had a chance to be mischievous again.

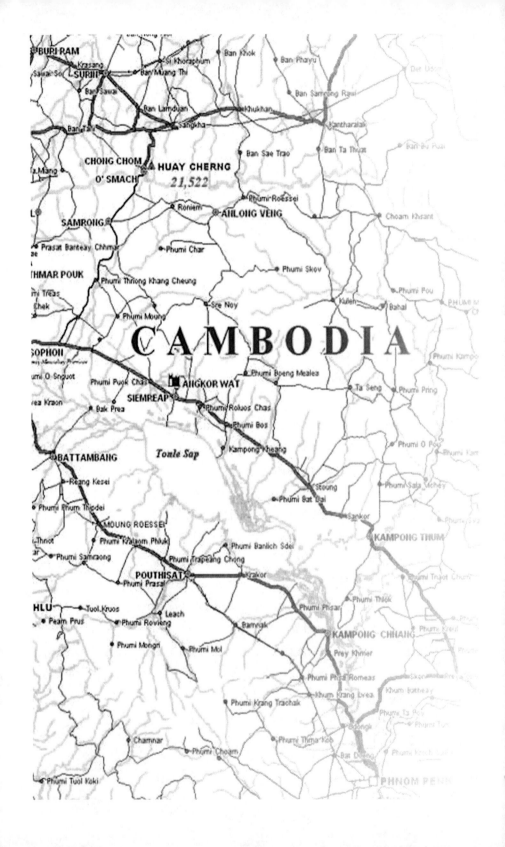

Part Two:
The Red

"Deliver me, O my God,
out of the hand of the wicked,
out of the hand of the
unrighteous and cruel man.
For thou *art* my hope, O Lord God:
thou art my trust from my youth."
Psalm 71:4–5

Chapter 10

The Horror Begins

On the evening of April 16, 1975, Maine and I were playing in an alley and were startled by the terrible sounds of bombs, guns, and sirens nearby.

In our young minds, it seemed like the gunfire was aimed directly toward us. In the following mass of people and chaos, my father managed to find us. When he did he leaned down to me and said, "Do not talk and do not ask questions. Do what the soldiers say so that we can stay alive."

Then—without warning—he pulled out a knife and quickly cut off all my hair. I cried out at the sight of my long hair falling to the ground. My father shushed me. I didn't understand what was happening or why my hair had been chopped off, but I understood one thing: I was supposed to remain quiet. We looked up to see a throng of soldiers headed in our direction. Suddenly we were sitting in front of a bunch of soldiers who were yelling at us as though we were animals. Then we began walking with a crowd of people, ushered by soldiers.

During our walk, we were told that the Americans were going to drop bombs in the city and that was why we had to leave. Therefore, members of the Communist Party of Kampuchea (CPK/

Khmer Rouge) had begun evacuating people from all of the cities in Cambodia.

In 1970, Prince Norodom Sihanouk, the leader of Cambodia, had been overthrown in a successful coup by Marshal Lon Nol and his pro-American associates. Unfortunately, their coup led to the rise of CPK support, and Lon Nol's regime ended within two years. Thus, the Khmer Rouge regime began. The goal of the CPK was to enact the "Four-Year Plan." The Plan called for the collectivization of all private property and placed national priority on the cultivation of rice to be used as an export. Although we did not yet know this information, we were to be involved in the Plan, and we were being taken to a place to work.

Traveling was slow, but my dad made sure we were all together. I held hands with my brother Maine, my dad with my youngest brother, and my mom with my younger sisters. My aunt had her daughter in her arms, and my grandmother walked beside her.

The streets were filled with a sea of faces. Everyone walked blindly ahead. Occasionally, people had to step off the street to let an army truck pass. Sadness was reflected on the adults' faces, children cried because of hunger and exhaustion, and little kids were left weeping in the streets as they searched for their mothers. I saw devastation in the children's faces. Streams of tears poured down their faces and snot drained from their noses. I was curious about the abandoned children, and I asked my father why they were left alone. He responded, "Their parents were probably taken by the soldiers." At that response, I began to cry, but my father reassured me with words of kindness and hope that God was watching. He reminded me never to forget what I was told about Jesus and that I should pray for Him to guide me. I was too young to understand what my dad was trying to tell me, but I could see his head bowed down and his lips moving in mumbled prayer.

After hours, we had only traveled a few miles when suddenly, I saw someone out of the corner of my eye. I looked back, and creeping up behind us was a Khmer Rouge soldier. I made eye contact with him and then quickly looked away, hoping he didn't notice me staring at him. He reached my father, jerked him aside, and demandingly asked, "Are you one of Lon Nol's soldiers?" He then pointed a gun at my dad's head.

"No. I'm not," my dad replied. "I am just a peasant man who works on a farm."

At that moment we were so scared for my dad. We were worried that the soldiers might take him away from us. My mother covered her face to hide her beauty because she was terrified to be seen. If anyone noticed her beauty, she would surely be taken away and raped by soldiers. My brothers and sisters could not stop their tears from coming. Though she was trembling like a leaf, my grandmother spoke up, "We all just work on the family farm growing rice and raising animals."

With that, the soldier laughed, "Where you all are going you'll sure be farming all right."

It was almost completely dark and we were hungry and tired, so our dad told us to stop and rest a little bit so the others could catch up with us. Our whole family was almost all out of energy. As soon as we sat down near a grassy area, we saw several dead bodies nearby. The people had died from multiple gunshot wounds and blood covered their faces. Their bodies were nude. There, in the grass, lay a small child, a man, and a woman who had probably been trying to run but couldn't make it. I was so shocked that I couldn't move my legs or cry. My dad said that we should not stop to eat and that it would be best if we kept moving.

We continued walking and the images of those dead bodies became an obsession clogging my brain. Questions flooded my mind. *Why was this happening? Where were we being taken? Were the soldiers going to give us a home? Were they going to feed us? Were we going to die from multiple gunshot wounds too?*

Chapter 11

The "Red" Camp

I t seemed like we had walked for days but had gotten nowhere. Then we heard the soldiers yelling for us to stop. And so we did. In this little place similar to a house, we saw a boy who was not much older than me. He was wearing a large, green camouflage army shirt that was way too big for him. The Red soldiers were yelling at the boy and whipping lashes into his arm. Then a Red soldier walked up to the boy, pulled him by the collar, put his pistol against the boy's head, and fired. The boy's head exploded and he fell to the ground. The Red soldiers then turned toward all of us and told us to line up. They commanded that if we did not listen to every word they said, the same death would happen to us.

Then they started to separate us children. They seemed to put the ones from knee to shoulder height together in one group. The other groups were adults, small children, and infants. There was mass anguish, and cries and panic filled the air as small children were taken from their mothers and placed in a group to themselves.

All I remember is my dad saying for me to stay with my brother. He told me that no matter what happened, from that day forward I was to act exactly like a boy. I was a boy from then on. He reminded me to pray to God and to believe in Him no matter how bad things got. I then said a prayer to myself, "Jesus, if you can see us or hear us, please help us. We are only children. Please let us see our parents."

My brother and I were placed in our group of all boys. I was relieved that I had pulled off the act of being a boy to the soldiers. Little did I know that I would have to continue the ruse for the next four years.

The following morning, I woke up sweating next to the rice paddy. The hot and dry season had just begun. In an old, abandoned building, there was a long hallway full of young and old people who were all caged like animals. All of us sat and ate on the floor. Everyone had to line up and catch the bowl of rice soup. Sometimes if one of us got lucky, we might get a bone.

The Khmer Rouge government called us *Angkar* or "The Organization." They wanted to provide for all of our needs. That way, the people would have to totally rely on the government. It was a method of control. Because all of us who worked in the rice fields worked exceedingly long hours, we were all exhausted and starving. For example, younger people—from ages six to 13—worked from 5 A.M. until midnight. At that pace, when all of us were lined up for food, there was not much left. Some of us were sent to bed without any food at all, crying from hunger and sheer exhaustion.

Starvation began to happen more and more. Some of the children died while working in the rice field. They fell flat in the mud, and their bodies instantly went limp. We all were forced to continue working, while their bodies floated around us in the muddy water. Some of us held in our crying because we did not want the soldiers to learn that we had any emotions. We were afraid that the soldiers would kill us if we did. This went on and on, and the adults couldn't do anything for us at all. They too would be killed if they tried to help.

If we were very good—if all of us children did perfect work and did not cause any disturbances—we would get permission to visit the next village where our parents worked. That meant that I got to see my family. On my first visit, I found out that my grandmother had died, and I could see my mother's face filled with sadness and fear. I asked my dad why this was happening to us. He told me that it was not our fault and that it was the fault of terrible men.

We got only about four to six hours of sleep a night. We worked all day. Sometimes we were afraid to sleep too deeply because we didn't want to get carried off in the middle of the night by soldiers. I would say that I worked 12-plus hours daily. I remember that we woke up before the sun rose, and we worked until long past sundown. I would say that it was until about midnight. And then we'd start all over again.

One evening after working in the fields all day, we lined up to get our rice soup. I remember being exhausted and feeling sick. An older woman saw the reason I felt so bad. I had a leech attached to my right ankle. It had been there for a while but I was unable to get it off. She sprinkled a mixture of something on the leech and gave me a stick to bite down on. Then she quickly cut the leech off my ankle.

We were forced to pee and poop in the field. We smelled so bad that the smell didn't bother us anymore. We couldn't go to the bathroom anywhere else because the soldiers wouldn't let us. If anyone did leave to go use the bathroom, he wouldn't come back. We learned quickly that we were never to speak unless spoken to or else we would be killed.

I wore a little button-up shirt. Though it had been originally white, it was so dirty that it was black. I wore a piece of cloth around my waist.

We called our camp the "Red" camp because each time we came back, someone had either been shot or had been hung on a post with blood dripping everywhere. Sadly, we had to work even harder during that time. We were not working in the rice field but were digging a hole instead. We called it "the Big Hole." At the time we didn't know what the hole was for or why we had to dig it. Eventually we learned that the Big Hole was a mass grave for all those who had died and were to die in the camp. Bodies were dragged out to the hole and tossed in. Lifeless limbs bounced off the bodies underneath, and the smell of death forever lingered in the air. The smell of rotting flesh was enough to make even a strong-stomached person sick.

Even people who were still alive were thrown into the Big Hole. It was a death sentence for those who were barely hanging on. The sick, the injured, and the elderly were brought to the Big Hole to die. The next month when we were sent back to work on the hole, there was no need. It was already completely full of bodies. It was so full, in fact, that heaps of bodies hung over the sides of the hole. By then the smell was so putrid that you had to hold your nose when you were near the hole to refrain from vomiting up whatever small amount of food you had in your stomach. I inhaled through my mouth and held my breath. At that very moment, a nearby soldier laughed and asked if I'd like to be thrown in the hole. I shook my head to say no, and the soldier continued his insane-sounding cackle as we headed back to the rice field.

We were urged to work harder and faster.

Chapter 12
My Favorite Number

A t our camp, you were not a name; you were a number. You were only one number in a long list of equally unimportant numbers. My "favorite number" was a small boy who seemed somewhere between my age and Maine's. I met him in the rice fields. I honestly don't know if the child was a boy or girl like me, but I assumed he was a little boy. Everyone in our camp was supposed to be a boy, but I knew I couldn't be the only one pretending. At that point, I had spent three years disguised as a boy, and I hadn't been discovered yet. If the soldiers ever found out, I would be killed or raped. But I was very malnourished and underdeveloped, so it was impossible to guess my gender.

At night we slept next to each other in the sleeping shack, and once every few days we were fed. The sleeping shack was not a shelter because it was outdoors. It was a two-by-four structure with a type of straw on top of it. It was just a shed.

We dreamed of big bowls of rice and told each other, "I'll give you half of it," and "I'll give you half too." Sometimes we'd catch a chicken.

We weren't allowed to call each other by names, so I never knew my friend's name. We just looked at each other, and we knew that we were friends. We were in the same boat.

We had a few more than 200 kids who worked in our camp. We started out with more kids, but each day the number dwindled to fewer and fewer and fewer. The soldiers randomly picked off kids one by one or sometimes two by two, and we never saw them again. I didn't want to know where they were being taken, though my only assumption was that they were probably taken to be killed. A lot of us believed that they took the boys to a group of soldiers. If the boys refused to comply, the soldiers would kill them. Every day the soldiers picked a number, and all you could do was hope that it wasn't your number.

My friend and I became so miserable that we wanted to die at the same time. We went out and found two large rocks. We held the rocks up close to each other's heads. Our plan was to hit each other in the head with the rocks as hard as we could at the same time, but we couldn't do it. All I can remember was secretly praying. And he would ask if he could pray with me. We looked at the sky and I told him to say what was in his heart. I looked up there and asked for protection and guidance and food.

One night my friend and I were so hungry that we ran out of the camp. We didn't know where we were going and soon we came across a cornfield. A bunch of other kids saw us run to the area and they joined us. We cracked open the ears of corn and ate like kings. We both were sitting there laughing at the fact that we were stealing food. We ate as much as we could eat. After we had finished, a gunshot went up in the air. We had been found. We ran in different directions. We were literally so scared that we all peed in our pants. You could smell the urine on us. The soldiers were screaming at us.

I closed my eyes and thought that I was going to be killed, but for some reason we were spared. The soldiers took all eight of us back to the camp. The next day we were punished very hard. We were forced to work for a week without getting any more rice soup.

The one special moment that we had was when we were eating that corn. And I will never forget it!

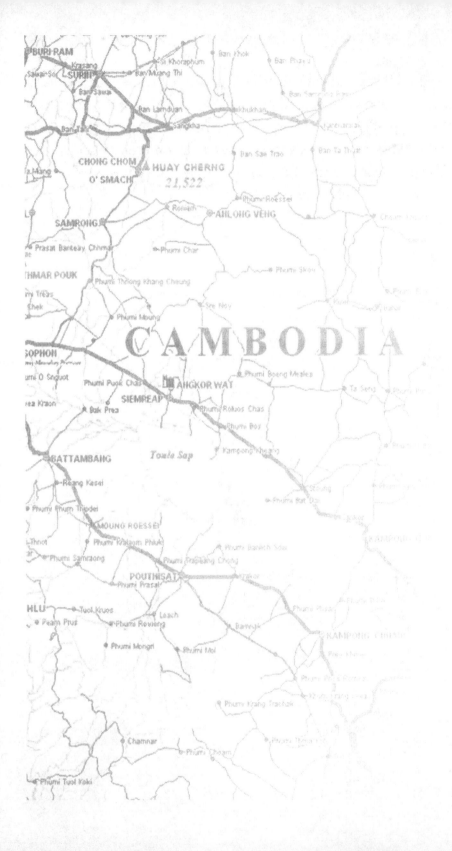

Chapter 13

Duck, Duck, Goose

After another 15-hour day in the rice field, we were taken out to a small bonfire in the camp. My young friend was with me, which made me happy. I was always glad to see him. We were told to sit in a large circle around the fire. I thought we must have done something right because only 20 of us were asked to go. It had been a long time since I'd seen a bonfire. It reminded me of better times when I had been with my family back home. Those times seemed like a lifetime away.

We all sat down on the ground. I looked into the eyes of a boy on the other side of the circle. The expression on his face made me think that maybe I was wrong about this fire. I had thought it was a kind gesture to those of us who had worked the hardest, but I could tell there was something that this boy knew that I didn't. He seemed to be holding back tears. I could tell. I knew I often had that same look of desperation on my face. But I also knew that if I cried, I'd be beaten or worse.

The officers began to shout at us, and it was then that I knew there was something horribly wrong. One officer pulled out a gun, and he began walking around the circle waving the gun out in front of him like a lunatic. He yelled, "Too many of you are weak! It is time for you to become men."

Become men? We were only children. Some of us weren't even ten yet. I inhaled deeply. I knew something terrible was about to happen. The officer held his gun up against my friend's head. I glanced over at him, but I made sure not to display my discomfort. The officer then moved over to me and held his gun to my forehead.

"Are you a man?" he shouted. I did not speak. From what I had learned in the camp, I knew that he truly did not want a response.

He moved around the circle. One by one children were questioned. I made eye contact with the boy across the circle. I could tell he was about to cry. I shook my head. *Don't do it. Please don't do it.* The Red officer got to him, and—without question—sent a bullet straight through his head. Many of us screamed in horror as the boy's lifeless body fell backwards into the dirt.

"You need to be men!" the officer shouted once more. "Tears are a sign of weakness! You are to be strong."

The officer moved around the circle again, faster this time. He held the gun up to each of our heads. And every few kids, he shot another one. Each round was more painful than the last. The children who showed the most weakness were shot first. If we lasted, that meant we had survived the test. After a few more rounds of horror, the officer stopped and directed us back to our sleeping quarters.

How were we supposed to sleep after that? What kinds of nightmares were going to haunt us if we could sleep?

Chapter 14

Maine's Story

I was working as hard as I could, but I could feel my weak muscles aching. At the same time, my brother grew exceptionally exhausted. I was working in a line that was near Maine's. I worked harder to pick up his slack. But I knew that the soldiers were fast approaching and he surely would be beaten if he didn't keep up. I watched as a Red soldier walked up next to my brother, and a long-growing fear became a quick reality.

The soldier pulled his gun from its holster, held it up, and hit my brother repeatedly on his back with it. Then he took the butt of the gun and hit Maine so hard in his back that it caused all of the kids to start screaming. Maine's screams were unlike any I'd ever heard him utter before.

I knew Maine was hurt badly, and without thought, I broke from my line and ran to his aid. I was on the sixth row and he was on the fifth. I was running through the mud, being chased by soldiers. Soldiers were on both sides of me and at the time, I didn't care if I were going to be killed. I did hear guns go off, but I don't know if they were shooting at me. I ran to Maine, and the soldier cocked his gun and pointed it at my forehead. "What are you doing out of your line?" he screamed.

"Please! Please don't hit him again," I begged. "Please don't hurt him anymore. I will do anything. I can work his line and my line, and I will give up my next few rations of food." The words came out of my mouth faster than I could even think about them. But I knew I had said the right thing.

I looked Maine directly in the eyes. His painful tears let me know that he was badly hurt, and the crook in his back indicated that he had broken bones. I nodded to him in assurance that he must keep fighting. The soldiers dragged him off and he was still alive. I knew that they weren't going to feed him and that he might be forced to lie in the pit with the dead. With that, I ran back to my position and continued to work.

Later I learned that my brother Maine was still alive though he was broken and weak. From then on, I had to work his and my row too but I didn't care. He was still alive and that's all that mattered.

Chapter 15
Chasing Tadpoles

By this time, there was less food each night. When night came, I was extremely tired after I had been in the hot sun all day. We were all so hungry that some of us decided to sneak out one night and catch frogs and tadpoles. We caught mostly tadpoles, which could be eaten raw, straight out of the water. When you're hungry enough, nothing tastes bad. You can eat anything.

Every night we had to sit near a fire with the soldiers surrounding us. They tried to convince us that they were some sorts of gods and that they were there to protect us. They told us that our parents were bad because they didn't know how to take care of us. I was too wise for the soldiers though. I knew that they were trying to brainwash us so that we would not want to see our parents. Some kids chose to do just that, and they got small rewards for it. My brother and I loved our parents too much for the soldiers' trick to work. All we wanted was the opportunity to be able to see our families again and to continue with the life we loved. Before we went to bed at night, we prayed for food and for our parents' safety.

Within the next couple of months, many old people disappeared at night. When night fell, fear and terror reigned. Many questions haunted my mind. *What was death? What did it feel like to be dead?*

Why did people kill? What was it like to be taken away and have your head shot off? Was I going to be the next person taken? I did not understand the reasons for taking lives then, and I still do not understand. And I am scared each day for the people around the world who continue a daily struggle for their lives.

I daydreamed about what it would be like to live in America. *Would I have a lot of meat to eat on a fancy table, the finest shoes, and the best clothes?* Of course, we did not wear shoes.

My dad was such a believer and he tried so hard to help Maine and me understand whom God was and why it was important for us to trust Him. When we got to visit our parents' camp, my father still tried to tell us about Jesus. But our faith-based discussions had to come to an end due to the increased fear of being caught believing in anything other than Buddhism. Our dad never could explain this too well, and now I understand why. Life wasn't the same inside the camps.

Chapter 16
Land Mines

After some time had passed, my youngest brother and sisters died of starvation, and my mom and dad seemed out of touch with the world. It seemed as though they both wanted to die together. My dad loved my mom so very much that I'm sure witnessing her abuse and not being able to do anything about it was difficult for him to bear.

The last time I saw my mother alive, half of her body was bruised and it looked like her back was crooked like Maine's. It was difficult to look at her once-beautiful face turned ugly by horrific abuse. I could barely look at my own mother. She showed no emotions. She had always been the type of person who never told you if she loved you or not. I wish she had been able to talk to me. I wanted her to tell me that everything would be okay and that we would be a family again.

All of us were walking back to the kids' camp about a half mile from another Khmer Rouge camp. Near the grassy open fields, there were kids in small groups under a tree for protection from the tropical heat. We watched those kids being slapped and some being sexually abused. We became afraid to approach this camp, and so we hid. However, if we hid too long, we knew that we would be punished for not getting back to camp on time, so we all took a different route.

We entered the open field and started running toward our camp. All of a sudden the ground around us started exploding. There were land mines everywhere! The explosions were so loud that I covered my ears with my hands and ran faster and faster. I thought we were all going to die, and some of us did. When we got to the camp, we were afraid that the soldiers would surely kill us all for not being on time and for taking a different route coming back. Once again God protected me and the others who had made it back.

Chapter 17

Starvation

I t seemed like days before we had anything to eat. Finally the soldiers gave us some rice soup. The kids cried at nighttime for food, so one night some of the older kids decided to sneak out to steal some food. That included me. We took off down a muddy path and ran quickly and quietly. Then we stopped. We had done it. We had found food. In front of us were rows and rows of corn. With the excitement of our discovery, we all started to peel the ears of corn and eat them right there in the field. After filling our bellies with corn, some of us packed more of it in our clothes so that we could give it to our siblings when we got back. I was shoving the last corncob in my mouth when I heard the terrifying sounds of a yelling soldier. He was right behind me, and there was nothing I could do but stare at him in agonizing horror as he hit me so hard with the barrel of his shotgun that I fell down. It seemed like forever before I was able to get back up. All of the soldiers were screaming and pointing guns at my head. *This is it for us. We're dead.* We were so scared that some of us even pooped in our pants. I know that I did. We stood by the corn awaiting our deaths, but instead we were told to return to bed.

For some reason we were not killed that night. Once again, God saved us.

The soldiers weren't "nice" anymore, and some of us were ordered to go to the building. The screaming that we heard coming from there wasn't good at all. Some kids came back and some, well, we didn't know what happened to them. I was praying to God and told Him that I didn't want to die then. I told God that I wanted to live and see my mother and father again.

Morning came, and I had been spared from being called to the building. It was amazing to me that I was still alive. The morning sun was brilliant. The birds were still singing, and I was still breathing. *How could this be?* I can barely explain how I felt. It was such an intense feeling of relief and I was thankful for a beautiful day.

A soldier came and took the rest of us who had stolen food the previous night to the other side of the camp. He took us to an area that none of us were too familiar with. We were chained together by our legs in the corner of the building. We were physically and emotionally exhausted from the heat, the lack of food, and the brutal surroundings. We had to live in that prison camp for a few months. During those months it seemed like I would never see my parents again because we experienced inhumane events that were almost too much to bear.

A few hundred prisoners attempted to escape and were all gunned down. Most were left in the open field to rot in the same places where they were killed.

Chapter 18

"No matter what happens, you need to stay strong."

E ven in the midst of our trials, I never stopped praying and asking for help. I was hoping and praying for some sort of miracle to happen. One evening, a monsoon had passed by, had left a tremendous amount of water in the fields, and had flooded the building. I heard the guard yelling that we had to move, so we were untied and moved to the next village.

In that village, I saw my father holding my mother in his arms. She was dead. Her lifeless body didn't even look like her. Uncontrollable streams of tears began to run down my face. I wanted to scream, but nothing came out. I looked at my father and said, "Dad, please look at me."

It seemed as though he was dead too, but he wasn't. He was in some sort of a trance, staring out into another world. He seemed stuck in that alternate world. I began to cry. And finally, he came to the realization of whom I was and broke from his meditative state of mourning my mother's death.

"Dad," I begged, "please help us kids, especially Maine. He is not well."

My dad looked up into my eyes for the first time and said, "Now I can lay your mother down to rest."

I looked at him and did not entirely understand what I was hearing. But in my later years, I realized that seeing me and knowing that my brother was still alive brought him back to reality. He looked at me sternly. Solemn meaning gleamed through his red, clouded eyes when he said, "No matter what happens, you need to stay strong."

Then he placed my mother's body carefully on the ground and covered her face with a small piece of cloth that he ripped from his clothing.

He then stood and took me aside. "Do you remember your aunt, Ly Pouy Houng?" he asked.

I scrunched my eyebrows and thought for a moment. "Was she the one who visited us and gave me candy?"

"Yes," he replied. "You must try to find her and she will love you as her own. If I am to die, she will be able to help you and provide a life for you." I looked at him with questions looming in my stare. I knew he saw my distrust in his statement, but he quickly continued, "You need to save your brother. Take him with you no matter what happens. You are his only hope for survival." He pulled me close to him by my shoulders. And with exhausted words, he whispered, "Promise?"

I promised him, *but what could I do? If my brother's time came, he would be gone. And then, I would have failed.* I thought about my aunt again. *How would I find her?* I knew my father must have been delusional. She could have been anywhere, and it had been years since I had seen her.

Chapter 19
A Little Ball of Rice

I t was time for my group to move on from the village. The soldiers also started moving the sick kids, including my brother Maine, from where they were to "a better place" as they called it. But the soldiers were liars. The new place was not better; it was much worse than where they had been. It was a dead place where they laid each of the kids, the elderly, and the injured on a grass bed to die. There was no medical attention or treatment offered there. There were only beds for those awaiting death. Some lying there were already gone, and their faces were covered with flies. I looked into the faces of the others awaiting death. Weary and saddened looks covered their faces. Their expressions let the visitors know that they wanted death, and they wanted it quickly.

A couple of days later when we got our little work break, it was time for our daily rice bowl back at the boys' camp. I sipped my soup carefully to make sure that I ate no rice. I poured the last rice lump into my mouth and formed it into a ball, which I hid in my mouth until I could reach the sick camp. I trotted off down the road, hoping that no one would ask me to speak so no one would notice the ball of rice in my mouth. I walked directly to where all of the dying people were lying on the grass beds. There were so many who were dead, were dying from diseases, had missing body parts, or had head injuries. The smells of death and of partial death loomed over them.

My brother was placed on one of the beds of grass, near an elderly woman on another grass bed. The woman looked able to speak and she tried to mutter some words. But her mouth was so dry that all that escaped from her lips were coughs of unrecognizable words. I walked to my brother's bed and found him in tears. He had been living like this for longer than I ever could have imagined he would have been able to survive.

There was a compassionate elderly woman walking around with a cloth and wiping off the faces of all those who were sick. She squeezed a few drops of water onto my brother's cracked lips, his lips finally parted, and he got a nice taste of water. Then I said good-bye to my last remaining sibling and assured him that no matter what, I would be there for him. I also told him that soon enough, I would have him able to walk again.

I kneeled down and acted like I was going to give him a kiss, and then I spat the ball of rice into his mouth, like an adult penguin does to its baby. Maine choked the rice ball down. It was difficult for him even to try to eat it because his mouth was so dry from his lack of water. Suddenly his eyes widened, and I swiftly turned around to see a soldier's raised hand. I barely had time to react before I was slapped so hard in the face that I saw black spots.

"What did you give him?" the soldier shouted.

"Nothing," I replied.

The soldier shook his head at me and then struck Maine in the mouth. I fell to the ground screaming. The desperate yelps could finally leave my lips, and I begged for the soldier to stop hurting Maine. The soldier lifted me from the ground by my arm, nearly yanking my shoulder out of place.

He yelled, "Return to your camps, and don't ever come back."

All of us visitors headed out of the sick camp quickly, and I could hear the soldier yelling as I ran, "If I catch you here again, you will be killed."

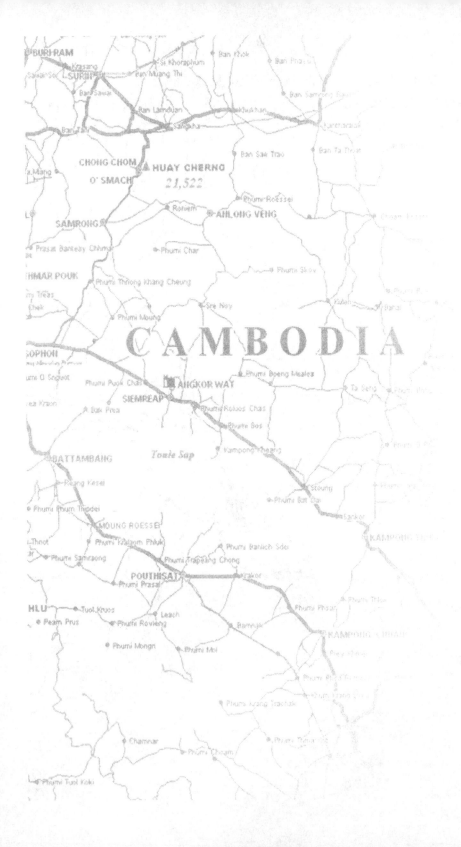

Chapter 20
The Escape

Several months later, I got to visit my dad who was very sick. His right leg looked as though the soldiers had shot a bullet into his knee and he was in a tremendous amount of pain. He didn't complain to me, but again assured me to "believe in the Lord Jesus Christ and you will go far."

I was very angry at everyone and everything, and so I asked, "How can you believe in a God whom you cannot see?"

My father looked at me and said seriously, "He is always with you, if you believe it with all your heart." As always, my dad said again, "Believe and you will go to a place called America."

I told my father that I believed but I wondered why God was taking so long to save us. I just didn't understand it at all. *Why—one at a time—was everyone close to me dying? Would he, Maine, and I make it out of the work camps alive?*

———— ∞ ————

Back at our camp at dusk, four men with ropes, guns, and bamboo sticks sat only yards from where I was chained. They waited for night to fall and then they took two other boys away. The Red soldiers did not use guns and bullets to kill passive, innocent people. Instead, they tied up the boys, made them sit next to the grave, and hit them on the backs of their necks with the bamboo sticks. Most of the time, the victims didn't die from the blows, but from suffocation afterward because they were buried alive.

That night I became out of it. I must have gone to that place in an alternate world where my father was after my mother had died. I was horrified that I would be taken next, and so I kneeled down, prayed, and cried. By that time, I didn't care if I were dead. I didn't want to live anymore because my dad was helpless and my brother was dying.

Having to act like a boy and live like a boy was also taking a huge toll on me. I had to bathe with men and watch them shower. I always bathed wearing whatever little bit of clothes I still had on. I was thankful that I had not developed yet and that I looked ugly so the soldiers couldn't even tell that I was a girl. I smelled so bad that not many Red soldiers even came near me. Sometimes they made fun of me and told me that I was ugly. I pretended to act dumb and did not say anything back so that they would leave me alone and go on to the next group of kids to belittle.

Soon after that, the soldiers came to me and told me that I could go see my father in the next village, and I was happy. But when I got there, my father seemed worried and tired. Flies were eating the flesh on his wounded leg. He whispered to me and told me that I needed to prepare to escape soon. And I was to bring my brother along with me.

Again—as I always did when I was a kid—I asked, "Why?"

My dad explained that the time had come to escape this horrible camp and go to a place called America. He and a group of men had already planned the escape. They had wanted to wait until the right time. And now that the right time had come, the others had told him that we would try to get out of the camp and escape that night. I was glad, but how was I going to get my brother and bring him along?

My father said, "At midnight, you meet us and you will follow us from there."

At midnight when the soldiers were asleep, one by one, we children tiptoed out of our camp. All of us hoped that we would not be seen. We started to run toward the adult camp so we could follow the men. I hadn't caught up yet because I had finally found my brother and let him lean on me with his hand on my shoulder. With Maine's broken back, it was impossible for him to walk. I hoisted him up on my back and carried him to meet with our father. At one point, my brother asked for me to leave him because he was in so much pain. I don't know where he was hurting, but he was definitely in pain. He looked terribly thin but his stomach was as large as a basketball. I had to urge him on and demand that he continue onward with me.

"I have to make sure that you will survive this because that's what Dad told me to do," I said to Maine.

Once we met with the adults, we ran to the province near the mountain. We had to run in a strange path to watch out for land mines. We ran and ran through the thick forest as fast as all of us could. We all thought that we were safe, so we stopped to get water.

My dad looked at me and said, "I think that we are close to the border of Thailand," but he was wrong. We were much farther from the border than he thought. As soon as everyone stopped to rest and get water near the river, a soldier appeared in front of all of us. Then we were suddenly surrounded by Red soldiers. There was gunfire. Everyone started running, and very quickly there were bodies lying everywhere. We were running every which way to try and get away, but we were cornered. Everyone was terrified of what was going to happen next.

Of course, my brother and I tried to reach our father, but he shook his head to signal for us to stop. His body language was telling us not to come near him or the soldiers would kill us. Our dad didn't want Maine and me to be tortured, so we acted like he wasn't even our father and didn't go near him. I tried hard not to look at him when the Red soldiers were yelling at, hitting, and shooting at the adults.

After we had been captured, we were literally stacked on top of each other inside an army truck. Some people suffocated from the lack of oxygen as bodies were placed on top of other bodies. The soldiers drove us back to the camp, and that's when the worst of their retaliation started.

They drove us to a wooded area that I had never seen before. This area had a small wooden house that was surrounded by soldiers on it. They stopped the truck and ordered everyone to get out. We all were crying because we did not know what was going to happen to us.

Chapter 21
The Punishment

The Red soldiers started to line up all of the men. Each man was stripped of his clothes, blindfolded, and whipped while all of the women and children watched. The soldiers began to interrogate each man in line as they whipped them one by one. They asked each man whom the leader was and started to torture the adults one by one. The soldiers forced the children to watch.

Commotion, screaming, and crying surrounded us. People begged for their survival.

The soldiers started with the first man in the line to try to get someone to talk. The first man was asked, "Who tried to lead you to escape?" The man didn't speak. Then the soldiers began to torture him by putting a drill to his ear and pushing its bit straight through to the other side of his head. Blood seeped out of his eyes through the blindfold as well as out of his mouth and ears. I became numb with shock. I could barely watch as he collapsed to the ground.

At first we didn't speak at all because we were in shock. Then the women and children were continuously screaming because they realized that they were helpless in this situation and they were losing the men whom they loved.

The officers approached the next man and then they interrogated him. He didn't talk, and the soldiers took out a strange tool that looked like clippers. They started cutting the man's fingers off one by one, demanding that he talk. After he continued to refuse to speak, a soldier stuffed a bandana in his mouth. The man eventually bled to death.

By that time we children couldn't even scream because we were in such a state of shock. Nothing more came out of our mouths when we tried. We could only gasp in terror.

When the soldiers got to our dad, I finally broke down and cried. I began to do all I knew that I could do at that point. And that was to pray and pray hard. I prayed to the God my father had taught me to pray to and to Jesus. I looked up at the sky and pleaded with all my heart, "God, if you're here now, please look after my dad and make sure he dies quickly. If there is any way possible that you can let us die easily, then please do it. Lord, I believe in you with all my heart and all my soul like my dad taught me." I did all that praying.

And that's when a jeep came and the commander said, "How will these people work if you kill them all?" The soldiers killed the guy before my dad in line and then they stopped.

I don't know how I felt about it at the time. I was glad that my father wasn't tortured, but I also thought that maybe it would have been better to die there than to live the life of a slave. The remaining men were taken away and put in tiny rooms. The soldiers held us back from helping them. Each room was about four feet by four feet in size. Four men were placed in each room, and each man sat in his own corner.

I did not get to see my father again until about six months later. The soldiers loaded us kids up and took us back to the horrible camp again. They hit me so hard one time that I think I passed out. I didn't even know where I was. I was hoping that when I woke up, I'd be in a better place, but instead I was in a dungeon. And we were forced to go work in the rice field again.

My dad died about eight months after the first escape attempt. I don't know how much the soldiers tortured him. I wasn't there to see the torture. I did get to see him about four times before he died. The last time I saw him, I knew he wasn't going to live much longer. He was very skinny and sickly, and he had internal bleeding. Eventually he died leaning against a cement wall. The chain was still on his leg when he died. There was another dead person in the cell with him. The two of them had been imprisoned together in a square cell that measured three feet by three feet. I don't know if the soldiers made them go to work in the daytime. My father had suffered for a long time within the walls of that tiny cell. I don't know when he took his last breath. All I know is that the last time I went there to see him, he had died. The soldiers didn't bother to remove the dead bodies. They kept my father's body locked up in that cell.

I tried to hold the tears back so the soldiers wouldn't see me cry. I couldn't scream. I couldn't say anything. I staggered backward and took off running to the children's camp. I sat for a long time. It seemed like the end for me. I thought *Well, now what? What am I going to do this time?* I was concerned about my brother because he was again in the horrible dead place, the place where all of the people were lying around waiting to die. And there wasn't much left of him either.

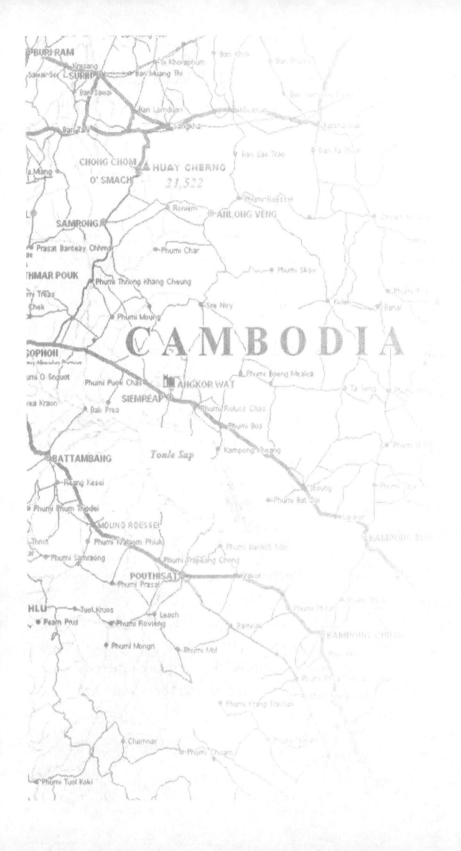

Chapter 22
Another Place

E ach day the soldiers took us out to the rice field to work. By that point my hands were so calloused from working that they no longer bled. I had shucked so much rice that I knew physical exhaustion was overtaking me. But I continued to work. I was working both Maine's duties and my own—as I had promised the soldiers—and it was becoming more and more challenging.

My muscles were no longer developing. Instead, they were stretching, which made it difficult to sleep the limited hours that I was given for sleeping. My legs ached at night as I fitfully slept. I found myself so restless on some nights that I could not even sleep at all. However my sleepless nights were not only from restless legs, but also from my ongoing fear of being taken away to another place in the middle of the night.

"Another place" was an area of mystery for those of us working in the camps. We assumed that when a person was taken away, they were to be executed. Rumors flew fast around the camp that when someone was taken to another place, the labor was more intense, the hours were never ending, and both eating and sleeping were nonexistent. Persons taken to another place were killed by being forced to work until they died. Some who survived the work camps were placed on the front lines of the war. There, they would surely die. Laborers taken away were never seen again.

It was my duty and my responsibility to keep Maine alive. My agreement with the soldiers was simple but extremely harsh to me. The soldiers would allow Maine to stay alive as long as I worked his weight and mine in the rice field. I was his only hope for survival. Long hours of working were imminent. We slept from around midnight until 5 A.M. and worked from 5 A.M. until midnight. Sometime between work and sleep, we ate our rice soup. As always, I hardened a small remainder of rice in my mouth and delivered it to Maine. Since my rations were smaller, his were too.

My "favorite number" and I had grown close over our time spent together in the camp. We developed a common bond since we learned that most, if not all, of our family members were dead.

One day when two soldiers came to our camp, I thought I was going to be taken away. A group of kids and I were lined up in a row. That meant that I was one of those selected to be taken away to the worst of all Cambodian labor camps, the Khmer Rouge camp. Since their takeover of the capital city, the CPK had a few main camps that were worse than the rest. The camp closest to Phnom Penh was known as the Khmer Rouge camp. We had only recently learned that this camp was what we had been referring to as "another place."

I stood in line next to my only friend I had made in our camp. The soldiers positioned themselves in front of us. One soldier was the selector and the other was his helper. The selector was the one who chose our fates. He was the one charged with giving us our death sentences. Then the helper grabbed the selected laborer and took him up to stand with the selector. Today, three kids were to be taken away.

The selector pointed his gun at the first boy in line, and he was taken to the front. I recognized that boy from the fields but did not have any personal history with him. The next boy was chosen from the other end of the line and was ushered to the front. The selector began walking in my direction. It was hard to keep a stern, unemotional face as he slowly approached my section of the line. *Please, not me. Please, please not me.* He neared my side and reached out his arm. I was sure I was going to be the one selected. But his arm slid past mine and grabbed the arm of my friend.

The two soldiers took him, my only friend. My favorite person was taken away from me. He was the only friend I had. *Why? Why? Why? Why did everyone I got close to have to leave or die?*

But my friend's number was chosen that day, and he was taken away. He never came back. I looked and looked for him in the fields, but he was gone forever. I never saw him again.

What was I going to do from then on? How was I going to make it without my "favorite number" from then on? How was I going to fight these people? It was impossible. I was only a kid.

I prayed every night. I wanted and desperately needed guidance from God. *How was I going to get out of the camp?* I thought about killing myself. At one point, I tried to get a kid to hit me so hard with anything that I would die. The child refused. Many of us didn't want to live any longer because life had become so horrible.

Chapter 23

Realization

My brother's condition worsened, and I knew that if I did not act soon, he would die in this place. I had nothing else but Maine to live for at this point. The only things keeping me together were my faith in God and my hope that my prayers would be answered.

By word of mouth, I learned that there were plans for a second escape attempt surfacing. As soon as I was certain, I headed quickly to my brother at the sick camp to get him and carry him with us on the escape journey that would hopefully lead to our freedom. When I arrived at the grass beds, the old lady was still there. She was continuing to wash the faces of the sick and to provide water to their thirsty mouths.

Simultaneous feelings of horror, disbelief, and anxiety resonated throughout my body as soon as I saw that my brother's bed was empty. I felt a tingle in the back of my neck and knew that the worst possible thing had happened. Tears began to fill my eyes, and the kind old lady approached me with a warm smile on her face. With one deep look into her caring eyes, I could tell that she had news for me that I was not prepared to hear. She leaned in close to me, held my cheek in her hand, and said gently, "I'm sorry, but he has passed."

I didn't want to believe her. I pushed her aside to run to the Big Hole, but I knew there were so many bodies that finding my brother would be a difficult task. All I wanted was to see his dead body. I needed reassurance and confirmation that he was actually dead before I could leave him behind. I had made a promise to our father that I would do whatever I could to get Maine to safety. This was the precise moment when I knew that I had failed to achieve the promised task.

The woman grabbed me by the shoulders and said urgently, "Go, and go now. This is your only chance. If you do not leave now, you will end up like him. Please believe me. He was taken to the Big Hole this morning, and he is gone forever. But you still have a chance."

I stared at her with tears of anger and remorse and asked, "Why won't you leave this place?"

She smiled her typical docile smile and answered seriously, "I am much too old now. There is no hope for me. I won't live much longer anyway. There is no reason for me to leave here. But, my child, there is a chance for change for you. And you need to take it. Now."

I was so frustrated. I had prayed countless times to the Lord to give Maine and me the opportunity to leave. If I wanted to survive, I had to leave without seeing my brother's dead body. That critical moment of decision will forever haunt me for the rest of my life.

I left the grassy beds and met the rest of the group at our designated spot. I had taken so long to get there that I was almost left behind. Since I had arrived, the group proceeded onward. When we reached the barrier, we took off running up the mountain. Just over the mountain was our promised land. We would be in Thailand soon if we kept hidden and moved quickly.

Chapter 24
A Moment on the Mountaintop

I stood just below the summit of the mountain. The group of refugees and I hid amongst the trees, waiting for just the right moment to race to our finish line, the Thailand border. Even in the coolness of the night, beads of sweat dripped down my face, and my heart pounded with anticipation and worry. I thought about my brother. *Where was his body now? Had I really left him behind? Was he really dead?* In my upcoming moment of escape, I had precious time. *But could I really believe what the old lady had said?* This was not the time to question myself. This was the time for concentration.

In a few moments, I would run through the forest with the others. Since I was one of the smallest, I would have to be quick to keep up with them. My lack of food already had left me feeling weak and feeble. As if my stomach weren't queasy enough, my recent actions of random hope for redemption had left bile boiling up my throat into my mouth.

I was suddenly jolted from my worrisome thoughts by the sound of a screaming baby. His piercing cries were sure to blow our cover. We would certainly be found if his hungering wails didn't cease. I watched his mother in panicked tears cover the child's mouth with her hand. Her breasts had already gone dry from starvation, and she was no longer able to provide for her young. She did the only thing a mother could do to save her own life. She smothered her baby to death. It was then that our group decided to travel down the mountain. Regretfully the woman wrapped her infant in a tattered piece of cloth and left him at the top of the mountain.

We quickly raced past the banana and coconut trees. Those trees had once meant food and playtime in my life, but as we ran, they filled my heart with devastation. *How had a place that was as beautiful as Cambodia been filled with such foul-souled scum?*

Suddenly I heard a noise. It was a loud, grinding sound that came from the sky. Though different from a seasonal storm, the noise reminded me of the terror that had instilled my surroundings on day one when we were forced to leave our home: the day after the parade. Just then, a helicopter loomed above us, and at that moment, I was sure it would be my last. A package dropped from the helicopter and dozens more packages followed. *Gifts? Could it be?* I watched cautiously as one of the men reached for a package. Just as he held it between his hands, it exploded in a cloud of dust and fire. All refugees who were nearby were blown back several feet. Those weren't gifts. They were grenades.

I couldn't run because I went into a state of shock. With my free land closer than ever, I begged God to help me to survive. Bombs blew apart on both sides of me and exploded those who once led me into these woods into fragments. My ears rang so loudly that I thought surely the explosions had deafened me. With more packages settling all around me and my head throbbing from my broken eardrums, I fell to my knees and began to cry.

I looked into the sky and remembered my father telling me "believe in God and one day you will go to a place called America and you will be free." I began to pray.

Still in my frozen state, I watched in wonder as a man in uniform suddenly appeared. His uniform was one I had never seen before. The man came out of the middle of nowhere and snatched me up. He ran wildly through the brush, shooting his gun in all directions as he ran. He managed to take out several Red soldiers. He was carrying a big bag with antennas sticking out of it on his back.

All of us refugees were separated, and I don't know if the others made it by different routes. I was too scared, so I wasn't looking closely. We were still several miles from the border with Thailand. It seemed like the man held me and ran for the longest time. He carried me until there were no bullets or gunfire. Then he put me down and we both walked toward the border.

All I remember is that I was with a person whom I'd never seen before in my life. I knew he was different. He looked different. He was kind with a gentle voice. I don't know what he said because I couldn't understand English at the time but I could tell that he was being kind. I never knew his name. But one thing I will never forget is the red, white, and blue flag with stars on his uniform.

When we reached Thailand, he kneeled down, handed me a small package, and patted my head. I looked down to open the package and when I looked up again, the kind man was gone. I never saw him again.

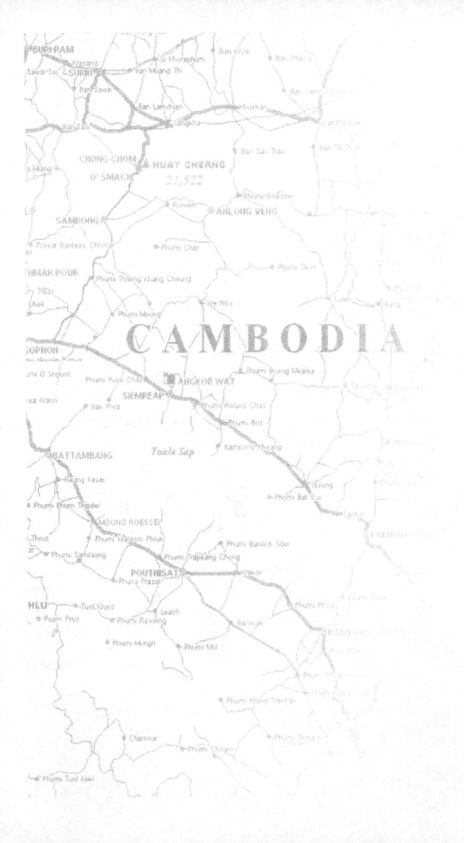

Chapter 25

The Safe Camp

I couldn't even believe it. I could not believe where I was standing. The realization of my successful escape was overtaken by exhaustion. Almost instantly I fell asleep. When I awoke, there were no soldiers. At least I didn't see any of them around.

I noticed a change in the people right away. Their behaviors were much different from what I had observed during the past four years of my life. People were actually talking to each other and engaging in normal conversations. There wasn't anyone going around hitting, torturing, or killing people. After having made these observations, I knew that this place was far better than where I had been living. But I didn't know where I was, where I was going, or what I was going to do there.

I noticed a line of people, but I didn't know why they were standing in line. It turned out that the people sitting at the front of the line were writing down refugees' names in order to figure out whom they were and where they wanted to go. The refugees waiting in this line were wondering if they were going to have the opportunity to be sponsored. To be sponsored meant that a foreign family or group was going to pay for a one-way ticket to the refugee family's desired location.

I realized that I was the only one by myself. Everyone else there was either in pairs or split up into families. I was all alone, and I had no one from my family left. Everyone had died.

I was also very nasty and covered in filth. I still wore the same outfit I had been wearing for years. At the work camp, I had been provided only one article of clothing, which had almost completely deteriorated and smelled dreadful. Without the foul odors of the Big Hole all around me, my nose was able to smell myself for the first time, and I smelled horrible.

I decided to stand in the line of people. In no time, I had reached the front of the line. I saw a person with a smile across her face. I was so used to acting rigid and unemotional that I'm sure I did not show any expressions at all.

"Name and age?" the woman asked.

"Lum Siv Lang. Fourteen," I sternly replied.

"And where would you like to go?" she asked.

I told her that I wanted to go to a place called America. At that moment the realization of my safety was sinking in, but I didn't know for sure where I was going to be placed or even if I'd be given the chance. After all, there were entire families trying to obtain sponsorship. I was just one person—one out of more than 80,000 people who were trying to be sponsored. The odds weren't in my favor.

There were thousands of people in the refugee camp. I didn't know what to expect or what to think. It was a shock to see people able to walk around freely, and I continued to look over my shoulder for soldiers to come. But none ever did. For the first time in four years, I heard children and adults chatting and laughing. There were no guns to be seen, and I knew then that I was safe.

For the first time in what felt like ages, I sat and waited for good food to be prepared. Once I received and ate my first meal, I nearly became sick immediately afterwards. Going from starvation to having plenty of food available sent my stomach into a state of shock. But I will never forget that wonderful first meal at the safe camp and my wide-opened eyes when I first saw that big bowl of warm rice. The tastes of that warm rice and—for the first time in years—actual meat enthralled me. The food melted in my mouth. It was the first time in four years that I had tasted anything other than plain rice in water.

At the safe camp, I ate vegetables including greens and one vegetable like broccoli. They offered a nice selection of meats to choose from including beef, pork, and fish. It took me a while to get used to eating more than one meal a day. I had been starved nearly to the point of death when I arrived at the safe camp, so my stomach had shrunk. It could no longer hold as much food.

I wanted more than anything to be one of the lucky ones. To be sponsored or loved by someone from another country was a dream that seemed far away. I thought I was never going to leave the safe camp, and I was scared because I was alone. If I went anywhere, I didn't know where it would be or whom I would go there with.

A few days after my arrival, I met an elderly woman. She had been widowed ever since the war started. A Khmer Rouge soldier killed her husband. I looked up to this lady. I had never seen her before, but there was something inside me that led me to her. Something felt right about my connection with her. She was soft-voiced and had a sincere smile.

"I wish I could provide for you, but that I cannot do," she said, shaking her head. A sad look crossed over her eyes and she looked away for a moment. Then she stroked my hair and told me to look up and that things would surely get better.

During my time at the safe camp, I came to know that I was really safe. I didn't have to fear the soldiers any longer. However, I felt more and more alone. I spent almost all of my time sitting alone and watching others. I was afraid that if I talked too much there, I'd be sent back to the work camp. I had lost all of my family. And for the first time in my life, I was truly all alone. And I was scared. *Would I be sponsored by anyone when I was alone?* I kept looking at everyone else around me interacting with others, coming, and going. I stayed by myself sitting and thinking all of the time. I was afraid that I'd be put in a work camp. And I thought about Maine. *What if I left him and he wasn't dead? What if he needed me?*

Most of all, I thought about where I might be going. *Was I going to go to a safe place? Or would I be stuck here at the safe camp forever?*

We lived in big, long tents in shelters at the refugee camp. At least we had protection from the weather. The people at the camp gave me clothes to wear.

Every morning, I looked at the long sheet of names of all of the refugees and where they wanted to go. If there was a check mark by my name, it meant that I had been sponsored. The interpreters at the camp encouraged me to be patient and told me that I would be going somewhere. They were very kind.

I had been in the refugee village in Thailand for about three months before the elderly woman approached me with the biggest grin on her face. "There's someone you should see," she said, and I followed her through the refugee camp wondering whom there was to see.

Around the next corner, I saw a lady standing with two little girls.

There was something familiar about the woman. Perhaps I had seen her en route to the camps or had played with her children before in the second village.

"This is the child," the elderly woman said, pulling me to her side. It turned out that the older woman had been speaking to this lady since I had arrived at the camp. She had been telling the lady how she felt sorry for me and that I was all alone. The woman facing me looked at me cautiously. She felt my hair and cupped my cheek in her hand.

"Lum Siv Lang, is that you?" the woman questioned tentatively. I could see tears forming in her eyes.

"That is my name," I said. I told her that my mother was fair-skinned and Chinese and that my father was half Cambodian and half Chinese. I told her about my name and that it symbolized the rarest flower in all of Cambodia, Vietnam, and Thailand. I told her what my grandmother had told me: that a person could look through the whole forest and only find one of these flowers.

It was at the very moment when I spoke of the flower that the woman began to cry and yelled, "Oh my God, you're my niece!"

That was the first time someone had recognized me as a girl since the day my father had cut off my hair. I felt an overwhelming sensation of shock. I wasn't sure what to do except hug her and cry. Her facial features were similar to before, just older looking. It had been many years since I had seen her. She was my aunt—my mother's sister. And out of all of the refugee camps in Thailand, she was living just two blocks away from me on the other side of my camp.

That reunion was one of the happiest moments of my life. My father was right after all. I did find my aunt, and she was willing to take me in as her own.

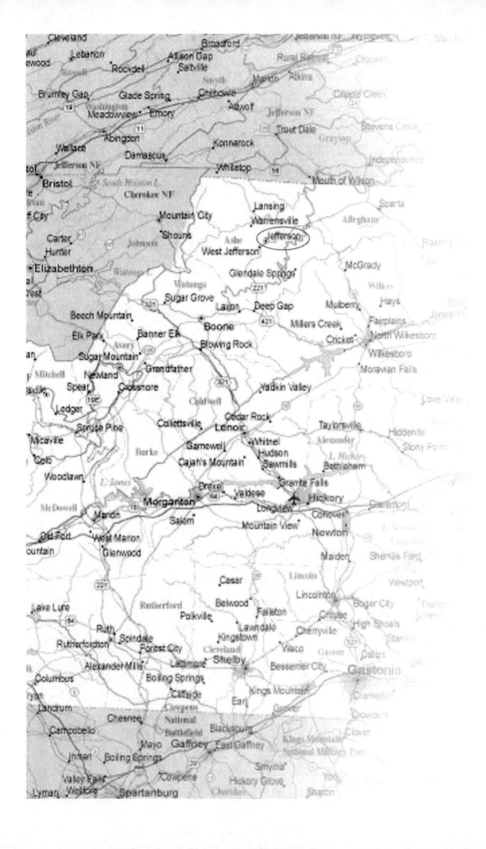

Part Three:
The Road to Recovery

"For God so loved the world,
that he gave his only begotten Son,
that whosoever believeth in him should not perish,
but have everlasting life."
John 3:16

Chapter 26
A Place Called America

What would seem worlds away in a town called Jefferson, North Carolina, a woman named Ina Ruth, the head of mission work at Jefferson United Methodist Church, and her colleague, Pastor Sweet, had been preparing to sponsor an adoption.

"What country are you thinking about?" asked Pastor Sweet.

Ina looked at the map, pointed, and said, "I'm thinking Cambodia."

"Cambodia?" Pastor Sweet looked at her like she was nuts.

Cambodia had been a war-torn country for nearly four decades. The year was 1979. Although the peak of the Khmer Rouge regime was over, Cambodia still had visiting restrictions and was a dangerous place to travel. Ina believed in her heart that God wanted her to adopt a family from Cambodia.

The sponsorship committee looked through thousands of pictures of Cambodian refugee families. For days Ina contemplated which family to choose. "How can I pick just one? There are so many," she wondered.

Finally, Ina came across a picture. There was something inside her that caused her to cling to that picture. She looked at the family: a mother, a father, and three beautiful little girls. They were framed in black and white on the long sheet of photos. Ina pointed to the oldest child in the picture and declared, "I want that child."

"Are you sure?" Pastor Sweet asked, telling her to be careful of her decision and to make sure she thought hard about whom she was going to pick.

"I don't need to think any longer," Ina said arguably. "The Lord has picked for me. He guided my hand to this photo, and there is something special about this girl. I choose this family."

The family in the photo was mine, and on July 10, 1979, we were told the news. We were going to a place called America, and I couldn't have been happier.

The next thing we knew, my aunt, my uncle, my cousins, and I were loaded into a van and taken to the airport. The airport was definitely the strangest place I think I had seen even though it would be considered a normal place to most other people. We spoke no English and were directed around the airport and onto the plane by a translator. The translator did not get on the plane with us, but she instead informed the staff whom we were and where we were going. They assured her that we would be safe and would arrive at our destination with little or no problem.

I didn't know what a plane was, and I was scared. Our family was alone and had no interpreter. I felt unable to communicate. The takeoff felt very strange to me. I'd never ridden in anything that fast before. Once the plane leveled out, I began to feel better about my safety. Instead of worrying, I waited in anticipation for our touchdown in America. We all sat in the same spots for 20 hours. I didn't know there was a bathroom on the airplane and neither did anyone else in my family.

When the plane landed at the airport in Charlotte, North Carolina, there were news crews filming our arrival. Jennie Hightower and Worth Sweet, the pastor of the church, greeted us when we got off the plane. Pastor Sweet was a big man, a very big man. He is about six feet, eight inches tall. He seemed intimidating at first, but we quickly learned that he was a sweet man, just like his name.

When we arrived in Charlotte, we didn't know what to do. We didn't have much of anything. All we had was one small bag that contained all of our belongings. One little bag for a family of five.

Pastor Sweet helped us get into the van that drove us from the airport. We eventually called him "Pappy." We had never ridden in this type of vehicle before. I kept looking at the things zooming by as we drove. We all thought the van was fast—I mean, compared to an elephant, it was.

It seemed as though the pastor knew that we were hungry. He stopped at one of the restaurants and ordered everybody a burger. We had never seen a burger before. He opened up the bun of his burger and squeezed a bunch of red stuff on it from a bottle. The red stuff was ketchup, of course, but we didn't know that then. Then he mashed the burger together and took a big bite of it.

"Mmm, mmh!" he said.

We started mashing our burgers too. And we made the same sound effects that he did. He got a real kick out of that. It's funny to look back now at our reaction to those burgers. We had never eaten anything like that before in our whole lives.

After eating, he drove us to a home in Jefferson, North Carolina. It was beautiful. We'd never seen a home like that before. It was a two-bedroom, one-bathroom mission home with a small kitchen and living room. It took a long time for us to learn how to use things in our new home. For instance, a church member showed us how to shut the door. It was something we had never had to do before.

There was one toilet in our home, and we had never used a toilet. We liked to flush it and stand around it to watch the water go down. We thought that maybe we were supposed to go to the bathroom outdoors, but there were often people around, so we couldn't do that. For a while, my mom used a bucket and water. Eventually a church lady showed us what the toilet was to be used for and how to sit on it.

For the first few weeks of living in our new home, we slept on the floor. The concept of sleeping in a bed was new to us, and honestly, we didn't even know what the beds were for. We were using them to store our clothing and had been sleeping on the floor next to the beds. After church members observed that we never had unmade the beds, they instructed us that beds were for sleeping by crawling under the covers and closing their eyes. We had a queen-sized bed, a bunk bed, and another small bed.

When we were growing up, we used our hands and chopsticks when we ate. At the work camp, we ate with our hands only. We didn't know anything about using the silverware that was in our new kitchen. When I went to school, people there showed me how to use silverware. I came home and showed our mom how to use it.

My mother didn't know how to use the stove, but church members were bringing us food all the time. Eventually they showed her how to turn on the burners and demonstrated how a burner worked by holding her hand above it so that she could feel the heat.

After we had lived in our home a while, church people gave us a TV set. All of us sat and stared at that television. We didn't understand any of what was being said. But we marveled when someone flipped through the different channels. There were so many different conversations. We walked around the front and back of the TV examining what in the world it was.

Once the weather started turning and winter settled in, we were baffled by the cold. It never got below 75 degrees in Cambodia, and that was on a cold day. We were getting along just fine with the colder weather until one day when it began to snow. Terrified for our lives, we ran indoors and hid under our beds. We literally thought the sky was falling. Pappy Sweet rushed over to our house as quickly as he could, knowing that we had never seen snow before. When he arrived, he found us hiding out, huddled against each other in a pack. He reassured us that it was okay, and one by one we came out from underneath the bed.

"See. It won't hurt you," Pappy Sweet said as he stepped off our porch and into the snow. It was then that we realized that snow was only frozen water.

Our first Christmas in our new home was memorable. Some church members came and put up and decorated a Christmas tree covered with glowing lights for us. We were fascinated by the tree. We all walked around the front of it and then around the back over and over to see those amazing lights. I plugged in the lights' plug, unplugged it, plugged it in again, unplugged it, and plugged it in again. I was just having fun. Finally my aunt told me to stop. She was afraid that I might break the lights.

Church members took us to see Santa Claus. We didn't know anything about Santa who was dressed all in red and had a long white beard. They wanted us to sit on his lap. But we didn't want to do that.

Before Christmas, a number of people from our church brought us beautifully wrapped boxes with big bows on the tops. We didn't know what these were or what to do with them, so we stacked them in our home. One day after Christmas, two church ladies came to visit.

They saw all of our unwrapped presents, and they decided to unwrap them with us to show us what to do with them. Unfortunately, the first present that we chose to unwrap was for one of my younger sisters. It was a jack-in-the-box. When the character popped out of its box, it scared all of us. Then we didn't want to open any more presents. We thought that all of them might be frightening like that one. The ladies realized why we were afraid, and they reassured us. They opened more presents with us to show us that the rest wouldn't scare us.

We loved our home and were very thankful for the opportunity that we were given. The photos below were taken upon our arrival at our home.

Chapter 27
Jefferson United Methodist Church

Our first trip to church was a learning experience. We didn't know what the building was used for but we knew it was beautiful!

The pastor said, "I'm the preacher," but we didn't understand what he was talking about. The pastor had a robe on and there was a big stand in front of him where he opened his book and read. That first week was when I heard the word *Jesus*. I couldn't communicate what that word meant to me, and Pastor Sweet couldn't understand why I was so excited when I heard it. He had no way of knowing that my dad had told me stories about Jesus after hearing them from the people whom he had met in Phnom Penh.

A year later when I could actually speak English, I was able to tell Pastor Sweet and other church members what my father had told me.

When I told Jennie and a lady we called Pretty Sharon, they had tears in their eyes. They elaborated, "We never knew that adopting a family would lead us to a child who had been taught about Christ already." Every Sunday those two ladies came and drove us to church.

Later I was baptized (sprinkled with water) at the Jefferson

United Methodist Church. Then I was baptized again years later at a Baptist church.

Chapter 28
My Father's Dream of Education

I started kindergarten at the age of 15 and completed high school within five years. It took a whole year to learn English. I was excited when I first went to kindergarten. The teacher didn't understand what I was trying to tell her about the American flag in the classroom. It was the same flag that I had seen on the uniform of the soldier who rescued me. Later, when I could speak English, I explained to her and my classmates why the flag meant so much to me. They finally understood what I had been talking about.

I was in a class made up of little kids. I had to learn how to read and write and speak English. The other children came to kindergarten knowing how to speak English. I think what the school, the teacher, and my classmates did for me was wonderful. If they had placed me in my own age group instead, it wouldn't have worked. I didn't know anything. I was exactly like a little child. I had to learn the basic things just like the other kindergartners did.

The other children took turns reading a book aloud to me, and I had to repeat it back to them. I didn't understand at the time why they read it over and over. Actually the reading was good practice for my classmates as well. Eventually I began to read.

I wanted to learn. For that first year, I was in school year-round.

The school staff moved me up from kindergarten through fifth grade. I worked really hard. Some church ladies were teachers, and they were willing to put their time in to help me learn. Sometimes I worked with two or three women at once on math. I was being moved from one class to another, so I didn't stay with any group of students very long. That didn't help me to establish friendships.

In my second year of public-school education, I completed the sixth, seventh, and eighth grades.

In my third year, I was a freshman in high school. I was in a much bigger school. That year was more difficult for me. Most of my teachers did not go to my church and did not know me. A guidance counselor was very supportive of me and explained to my teachers that I had just learned to speak English and that I was trying very hard in my classes. I was not a top student, but I was average.

In my fourth year, I skipped my sophomore year and was a junior in high school.

During my fifth year, I was a senior. I received my high school diploma five years after I started school.

This is a photo of my kindergarten class. I am on the second row at the far left. My younger sister is seated second from the right in the front row.

This photo shows me (top), my father and mother (left), and my three sisters (right). The youngest child in this picture was born a year after our arrival in America. At first, my mother kept her pregnancy a secret. Then one day, church members stopped by and my mother had another child in her arms. They were surprised at how well my mother and the baby were doing.

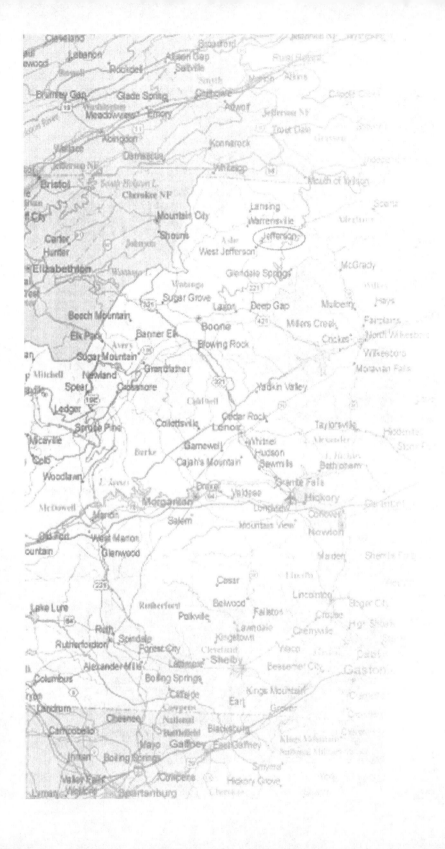

Chapter 29
Kenny and Community College

I always loved school. I was so thankful for the opportunity to learn that I didn't ever want to have to leave. After I graduated from high school, I decided to go to Wilkes Community College. I was 21 years old when I started classes there in October of 1986. That's where I met Kenny.

He says he saw me around the campus but couldn't get up the nerve to talk to me. One night we both went to a Halloween dance. I was sitting with my girlfriends.

Kenny came up, looked at me, and asked, "Would you like to go dance?"

My Korean friend shrugged and we looked at each other. "Are you asking me?" I asked.

"Well yes, I am," he replied. And I responded, "Sure."

I remember that I had dressed up as Medusa. I had made my costume, hoping that I would win the costume contest that was being held that night. Kenny hadn't made anything. He went home, put on a sheet, and wore tinsel around his head. And he came in second place in the contest. He was wearing flip-flops, and he placed higher than I did in the contest. That was the start of a wonderful relationship between us.

I had dated before I met Kenny but he was different from the rest. I loved him. We dated throughout our time at Wilkes Community College. In 1988 I graduated with two associates degrees from Wilkes. One degree was in art and the other was in hotel/restaurant management.

Chapter 30
Makoto's

L ike me, my uncle (who was now my dad) had an avid interest in cooking and foods. He soon became the head chef at Makoto's Restaurant in Boone, North Carolina. That worked out great for me, because Kenny and I both had decided to transfer to Appalachian State University in Boone to obtain our bachelors degrees in marketing.

I was extremely fortunate to have a job at Makoto's in Boone. I always got there way before anybody else. My supervisor liked my work ethic, so he promoted me and increased my pay. I was making a very good salary working there full-time while trying to be a full-time student as well. Doing both well was very hard on me. When I was offered the opportunity to take a management position at the Makoto's Restaurant in Johnson City, Tennessee, I dropped out of Appalachian after attending there for eight months.

I regret not having finished college, but I have come to know that God had a better and different plan for my life. Had I finished school, I never may have had the chance to write this book and to be able to have the time to give speeches and do other things related to my experiences in Cambodia as I can do now.

I was still dating Kenny when I moved to Tennessee. Eventually he also moved to Johnson City so that we could be together. I had worked at Makoto's in Johnson City for a year and a half when we learned that Kenny's mother had passed away in North Carolina. After her funeral he returned to Johnson City, told me how much he loved me, and asked me to marry him. I said yes!

In June of 1991, Kenny and I were married at the same church that sponsored my family. Soon after that, we moved back to his hometown of Hamptonville, North Carolina, to live close to his father.

Each day is such a blessing, and I am forever grateful for God's grace.

This is our wedding day on June 1, 1991, at Jefferson United Methodist Church.

Chapter 31
The Nightmares

When I first arrived in the United States and lived in Jefferson, North Carolina, I had nightmares or what some might call night terrors. When I had a nightmare, I ran down the street in a dreamlike state. Mama panicked and called Ina Ruth's daughter. She had to come and get me in the middle of the night and take me home. When she got me home, I would be sweating. The next day, I didn't remember a thing about what had happened.

In my nightmares, I always dreamed the same thing: I kept reaching for someone. It looked like a human figure. I think it was my brother or my dad. I woke up screaming.

I got some counseling to get help for my nightmares. They told me that I needed to let go of my fears. They really didn't help me at all.

I had tried to block out everything that had happened to me, but the trauma was too much, too deep, and too painful to bear.

Years later, Kenny woke me up and told me that I was screaming in my sleep. At first, I told him that it was nothing. I said it was "just a little nightmare." He accepted that answer and went back to sleep. I had been married to Kenny for around two-and-a-half years before

I ever told him about my experiences in Cambodia.

One cold night, during a highly delusional night terror, Kenny found me on the side of the road. He thought at first that I was crazy. It was at that moment that I knew I had to make a major confession to him. And I knew it was going to be heartbreaking for Kenny. I sat him down on our bed and took a deep breath before I began to explain the most difficult time in my life. I began with my family background and summed up the Red Regime as quickly as I could. I burst into tears because this was the first time I had ever told someone so close to me about the terrors of those four awful years of my childhood.

I told Kenny that before the work camps, I lived a life like every other normal child. I really loved and enjoyed the company of my family. During and after my years spent in the work camps, I had been hurt so many times that I didn't want anybody around me to get really close to me. The thought of getting attached to someone and losing him or her again was agonizing. I just didn't want to get hurt like that again.

Kenny listened intently to me. He hugged me tightly that night, and he made a promise that he would always be there for me whenever I needed to talk. "Why didn't you ever tell me this before?" he asked, squeezing my hand tightly.

I told him that I had been afraid that he would think differently of me if he knew about my past. And I told him that my tragic history did not define the person whom I am. However, that was much further from the truth than I thought. Once I began telling Kenny my story, my pain began to lift. My dark secrets were no longer stuck deep in my subconscious mind. I had brought them out into the light and had forced myself to face my past.

My realization that speaking openly about my past was not only helpful, but also necessary to my recovery occurred to me after I had given my first speech at Jefferson United Methodist Church. That speech was the first time I spoke about my past at any church. After I started telling the real story of my past, I never again had the nightmare about reaching out to someone.

Kenny was always there to support me. No matter what, he was there for me. Over time—as the counselors had advised earlier—he was also able to encourage me to let go what was buried deep inside me. Still later, he advised me to tell others about what had happened to me to continue to promote my own healing.

Chapter 32
Tia and Ty

K enny and I were planning to have children. We wanted children right away. However, I didn't end up getting pregnant until I was 29. We had been married for three years before this happened. My pregnancy was very difficult. After a complicated delivery, we were blessed with our first child.

Tia Shanelle Ashley was born on February 17, 1994. Kenny picked Tia's middle name after he heard the name of the popular perfume, but he wanted to spell it with an *s*. Later he decided on her first name being Tia because he had seen several movies featuring an actress named Tia.

My difficulties during my pregnancy and delivery could have been related to my physical abuse, long work hours, starvation, exhaustion, and underdevelopment during my four years at the work camps. I didn't tell my doctor about these experiences in my past.

After the difficulties during my pregnancy and delivery, the doctors told me that my body would be unable to handle having another child. I decided to be placed on birth control to prevent another difficult pregnancy. However, in the summer of 1995, I went to the doctor after having some stomach pains. I found out I was pregnant again, and I began to cry. I was afraid that this pregnancy would kill me or that there would be complications that could cause harm to the baby.

The doctors placed me on bed rest for my entire pregnancy. That was a tough time for Tia who was only about 15 months old when I found out I was pregnant again. I could not hold Tia on my lap during the bed rest. And it really wasn't fair to little Tia. Her brother, Ty Walker Ashley, was born on February 10, 1996.

I chose Ty's first name. Kenny picked Ty's middle name after watching "Walker, Texas Ranger." He decided that Walker was a good middle name.

The Lord has been good to me. I couldn't have asked for anything better. I thank God for giving us Tia and Ty. Originally I wanted five children because my real, biological family was made up of five siblings. Things worked out the way they were supposed to though. After Tia's birth, I thought I was only going to be able to have one child, but we were blessed with two.

Now Tia attends college in Western North Carolina and Ty is one of the smartest in his class as a junior in high school. He plans to go to college at Wake Forest University.

Chapter 33
Going Back

I n April 2010, my aunt wanted all of us to go back to Cambodia to resolve our issues with the area. Part of me was scared to go, so I kept telling her that there was nobody there for me and that there was no reason for me to go. But she remained insistent.

I went strictly to achieve some sense of closure. We visited her husband's relatives who lived in small villages throughout the country. Unfortunately, that was difficult for me. During the whole trip, I watched other people together as families. That only served to remind me that I no longer had any living family members. I grew more and more depressed as the trip wore on.

Although my aunt had wanted me to go in hopes that maybe we could find Maine, we didn't try to figure out anything about my brother. That would have been like trying to find a needle in a haystack. Even if he were still alive, he would have been impossible to locate.

My aunt wanted us to go and visit the two villages in which I lived when I grew up. I didn't want to go with her to either village. I didn't want to see where our family used to live.

We visited Cambodia for about three weeks. I missed Kenny and my children.

I was very relieved to come home. However, I came home with an empty heart, because I didn't achieve any sort of a sense of closure on the trip. I didn't feel like the trip had done me any good. I never dreamed of going back.

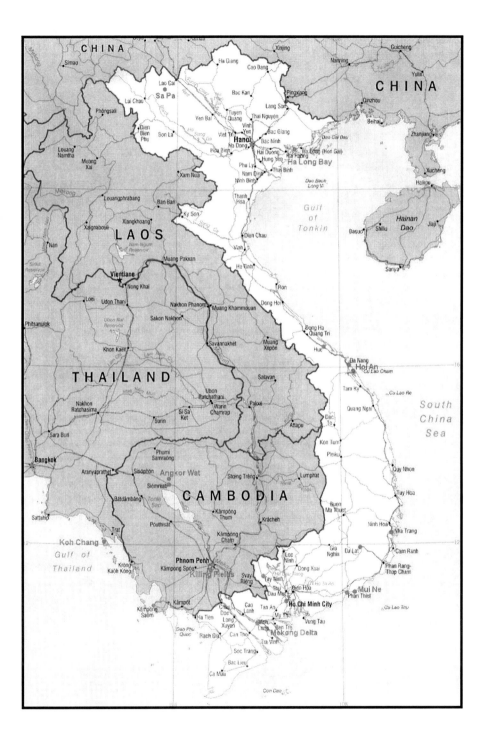

Part Four:
The Mission

"And he said unto them, 'Go ye into all the world,
and preach the gospel to every creature.' "
Mark 16:15

Chapter 34
The International Commission

I had been invited to a women's conference at Friendship Baptist Church in East Bend, North Carolina. Lena Church had mentioned me to Marci Hamlin and Marci had invited me to come and give a speech. Marci had also invited a woman named Donna Freeman to come and listen to me. After I shared my story, Donna came and shook my hand and almost cried. She told me that her mission team from the International Commission was going to Cambodia and that she wanted me to meet her team and go on the mission trip with them. She gave me a brochure and we exchanged phone numbers.

Three days later, Donna called me. She said that her team met every Sunday night at Jeff and Jodi's house, and she invited me to meet with them. I told Kenny after that call that I wasn't sure about the mission trip. I was sort of scared.

I couldn't join Donna's team on the first Sunday because I had plans at another church. The following Sunday I went and met with them. I started telling them about myself and told my story in about 45 minutes. They explained that they were planning to go to Cambodia in October. I wasn't sure if I could go or if I even wanted to go back again. I told them that I would have to get off work, get my family organized, and get my money together. They all looked at me and said, "With God, nothing is impossible."

As I was leaving, Jeff asked me to point out the place from which I had escaped on the map of Cambodia. When I pointed to the place, his face glowed with amazement. The area from which I had escaped was the same area where they were going to share the gospel.

The next day, a man named Scott Hubert called me at work and told me that he wanted me to go to Cambodia with the mission team. He said that he was going to raise the money for me. At that point I realized that this was real and that I was going back to Cambodia.

By the end of that month, Scott and others had raised all of the money needed for my trip. My supervisor at my new job agreed that I should go. It was amazing how the hand of God brought everyone together to make the mission trip to Cambodia possible for me. I felt much better about going this time around. I felt like I had a sense of purpose with this team.

It was all God. It was God who reassured me that I'd be fine and that I'd be able to tell people in Cambodia about Him.

Chapter 35
A Red Soldier's Redemption

T here were 27 people on our mission team. I arrived in Cambodia on October 16, 2012. I had to fly on a separate plane because I was the last one to sign up for the trip. We took a lot of Bibles to hand out while we were there. They were printed in two different languages.

I was happy to be on this team. I felt far more cheerful and alive than I did on my first trip back to Cambodia. I had a purpose on this trip.

We traveled by vehicle for three hours to reach the first group we visited. It was at a church, which looked like a little shack. The preacher gathered everyone around for us to talk to. There were about 60 Cambodians there. When I told them where we were from and that we were there to tell them good news, their eyes lit up. One of the little kids raised his hand and said that I looked like them.

Before I started, I explained to them that this was my first time telling this.

I told them the story of creation and about whom Jesus was. We had two pictures: one of heaven and one of earth. Then I told them my personal story about how I was just like them, how Red soldiers had killed my parents, how I had escaped from the work camp, how

I had reunited with my aunt, and how I had moved to the United States.

The preacher looked at me, put his hand on my shoulder, and told me through the interpreter, "I'm so sorry." He then went on to tell me that he was one of the soldiers from the Red army. He said, "Fifteen years ago I found God, I was saved, and now I am a preacher." The interpreter told me what he said.

I had no idea what to say. I was stunned for a minute. So was everyone else who was listening. And everyone was waiting to see what I would do.

Through the interpreter, the preacher asked me to forgive him. Again I was utterly shocked. There was another strained moment of silence. Then I told him that I had forgiven everyone who was involved for their actions—even those soldiers who had murdered many people including my family.

I said, "I'm glad that you came to me and told me that you were one of the soldiers. And I'm also glad that now you are with Christ and you go spread the gospel."

He was amazed that I could forgive him. I wasn't mad or angry. I was actually still shocked. I had expected Red soldiers to be alive. But I never would have expected for one of them to be a preacher, much less a preacher at the church I visited on the first day of my first mission trip. Without the love of Jesus Christ, I never would have been able to forgive him.

That's the reason I went on that mission trip: to tell the gospel. Because of Christ, I was saved.

Fifty-seven people asked Jesus to come into their hearts and were saved that day.

The Cambodian preacher/former Red soldier

Chapter 36
The Serpent

One day we went to a school that had about 700 kids in it. We gathered them all together underneath a tree, and I told the same story of creation and showed them pictures. The pictures were of Adam and Eve. I told them about the tree of knowledge and how the devil was a snake that tempted Eve to eat the fruit from the tree. As I was telling this, one of the little boys started yelling and pointing at the tree. I looked over there and sure enough there was a snake hanging in the tree. I looked at the kids and said it was OK. I told my translator to tell the kids to focus on me and that I'd stomp the snake if it came out of the tree. After I finished the story, the snake receded into the tree. The symbolism was amazing. I can't believe that snake was actually there at that particular time. It was phenomenal.

Seven hundred and one people at the school accepted Jesus into their hearts that day.

Chapter 37
The Saving Doll

We brought around 30 dolls to children in Cambodia to teach God's message. The dolls had closed eyes on one side and open eyes on the other. When they were with Jesus, their eyes were open. And when they weren't, their eyes were closed. Each doll wore a necklace with six beads representing different elements of Christianity. The beads were six different colors: black, red, white, blue, green, and yellow. The colors symbolized the following:

> black—for evil and sin
> red—for the blood of Jesus Christ that was shed for us
> white—for the purity of heart after we have received Christ
> blue—for the symbolism of baptism
> green—for telling and spreading the gospel
> yellow—for when we die when we will see God and that we
> will be with God in the end

For the next couple of days we went to more schools. We gathered the children right in front of us and let them sit on the red dirt ground. I was the one who showed the boy and girl dolls. I told the children about heaven and earth and the creation story. Then I held the two dolls up and told the children that when we know God, we are very happy and our eyes are open. I described all six of the beads and what they meant. Then I asked the group if they understood what I had said. They all raised their hands.

"Which one of you would like to come up and explain what I have just told you to everyone?" I asked.

No child raised his or her hand. I gave them another chance and encouraged them, "Don't be shy."

A little girl who was sitting there raised her hand. When I called on her, she began to tell the story. She described all of the beads. Tears poured down from my eyes. She explained that she couldn't afford to go to school. She was not even a student at the school but she had come to listen to us. I gave her the girl doll because I felt that she deserved it after having the nerve to get up there and tell the story in front of 900 kids. I gave her the doll so that she could go and continue to spread the gospel.

Later on, the little girl's mom came to me and thanked me for the doll. She said that she was half Chinese and half Cambodian too. We both started talking in Chinese to each other. That was too good to be true.

In a place where I had spent four years witnessing untold horror and bloodshed, God's presence was all around us during that mission trip.

Chapter 38

Moving On

More than 12,000 people accepted Jesus Christ into their hearts while we were in Cambodia. Most of them were children ranging from the age of six up to high-school age. The people in Cambodia were so humble and welcoming. They were willing to sit outside in the dirt to hear the good news of Jesus Christ and accept Him into their hearts.

Team "Jesus"—our mission group

I think often about my father's deep faith. No matter what, he never stopped believing. Years ago in this same country, we had to keep our faith in Jesus a secret. I am thankful that God gave me the chance to go back to Cambodia the second time to share my story and most importantly, to share His story of love and forgiveness.

I am thankful to the International Commission for all of the help and donations so I could go.

I loved my father very much. He loved all of us very much and wanted the best for all of us. My father had a number of goals that he wanted to see me accomplish. I have tried hard not to let him down.

He wanted me to escape from the work camp.

He told me to find my aunt and let her accept me as her own.

He encouraged me to always believe in God and Jesus and
   to pray.

He told me that I would one day go to a place called America.

He wanted me to get an education.

Remember to look to God, not just because something bad happens, but because He is there for you every second of every day. Don't ever lose faith in God.

Hebrews 11:1 (NIV) says, "Now faith is confidence in what we hope for and assurance about what we do not see." That's the faith my father taught me about. I thank God every day for my life. Because of Him, the blessings outweigh the pain.

A Lesson in History

The Cambodian Civil War is a war that has not been covered heavily in school or in programs. However, thousands of people were killed and lives were shattered for nearly four decades, making the Cambodian Civil War one of the longest and deadliest wars in history. In similarity to the Holocaust, the Cambodian Civil War ushered genocide into the nation and forced people to work for no pay and small increments of food. In contrast to the Holocaust, the genocide that occurred was not specific to a certain race or type of people. It involved the systematic killing of all parties unable to work.

Fortunately, the war in Cambodia did not spill into other surrounding nations and only affected the people of one nation. However, because the war lasted for an extended number of years, multiple generations of people were murdered and entire families were terminated from existence.

CPSIA information can be obtained
at www.ICGtesting.com
Printed in the USA
FFOW02n1608291017
41594FF

9 780984 672448